Sharpshooters & Sermons

The Parables Of Wrestling & Religion

Darren Kane

Forewords By
'Bravehart' David Low
And
Paul Clancy

*To Lesley
The Best Boss In The World!
Enjoy the book. I think you will learn a lot!
Darren Kane*

Sharpshooters And Sermons

Legal Notice and Introduction

©2015 Darren Kane and Manifesto 4:13 Productions
All rights reserved. No part of this book may be reproduced for commercial use without permission in writing from the publisher, with the exception of quotes and scriptures.
All scriptures are taken from the King James Version of the Bible, the Book of Mormon and the Doctrine and Covenants.
All photographs are from the authors own collection, unless otherwise stated.
All names mentioned (other than those from scripture and from wrestling television shows) are used with their permission.

Although written from an LDS member's perspective, this book focuses on Jesus Christ and Christianity as a whole. Latter-Day Saint customs and principles are used to illustrate various points throughout the book.

The wrestling stories come from WWF/WWE from a number of different years. This writer has been a loyal and avid follower of the company since 2000, and knowing that period of history well chose to focus on this era in most stories contained here. This writer confirms knowledge that wrestling is scripted for our entertainment, and the wrestlers themselves are working together to give us the best show possible. The stories told in the book are a mix of real life stories and that which is provided for our entertainment.

This book is not affiliated or endorsed officially by The Church of Jesus Christ of Latter - Day Saints, the WWE, any other Church or wrestling company.

The opinions expressed are the writers own and do not constitute official Church teachings and doctrine.

Contents

Acknowledgements..7
Foreword – "Bravehart" David Low............................11
Foreword – Paul Clancy..15
Prologue..17
Chapter One – "This Is Going To Be Art!"..................23
Chapter Two – "You're Learning From The Best!"......29
Chapter Three – "Try Not To Go Over The Top!".......36
Chapter Four – "Remember The Moments!"..............41
Chapter Five – "Prelude To Victory"..........................48
Chapter Six – The Omega Lineup..............................53
Chapter Seven – "Do It My Way!".............................58
Chapter Eight – "Bret Hart Came Home"..................64
Chapter Nine – "You Are The Legend Makers!".........76
Chapter Ten – "Be Sure To Catch Me!".....................86
Chapter Eleven – "If You're Afraid"...........................91
Chapter Twelve – "Having Been Commissioned".......95
Chapter Thirteen – "Like A Dormant Volcano".........105
Chapter Fourteen – "Your Tag Team Partner"..........115
Chapter Fifteen – "Light vs Darkness".....................121
Chapter Sixteen – "If I Can't Beat You!"...................127
Chapter Seventeen – "I'm Sorry I Let You Down".....138
Epilogue..144
The Make-A-Wish Foundation..................................149

Card Subject To Change

Sharpshooters And Sermons

Acknowledgements

First of all, I thank you, the reader for spending your hard earned money and your invaluable time to buy and read this book. A lot of time and late nights have gone into this work, and to have it read by an audience is the greatest blessing an author can receive.

I would like to thank Paul Clancy and 'Bravehart' David Low for contributing their thoughts into the forewords. I have known Paul through the Church for many years, and he along with his family have become very good friends to me. Paul's knowledge of the scriptures is so wide and precious, he has always been a joy to learn from and talk with. I thank him as well for the proof read of this book, ensuring all doctrine and scriptural references are correct.

I have known David since attending my first SWE show in Dundee, Scotland back in August 2011. We became friends straight away, and have had many talks since then regarding wrestling and our Religious beliefs. He is one of the greatest men I have ever met, and inside the ring he is a fantastic character and wrestler that is always a pleasure to watch, support and cheer on (and as he plays the bad guy, I am apparently his only fan!). His foreword really touched my heart and I am forever grateful to him for the important contribution he has brought to this book.

A special thank you goes to my good friend James Clancy. We went out for dinner one night and through reminiscing about some great wrestling moments the idea for this book was born. Thank you for your continued support and accompanying me to many great wrestling events over the years. We always have the wildest time.

   I'm grateful to Paul Roshier, for the outstanding cover he has contributed. When I spoke with him and explained what I was looking for, I was hopeful. However, when he sent it over to me I was so impressed – it was even better than I expected. He is a very talented man, and does many graphics and posters for the SWE.

   I'm thankful for the people of Amazon for providing this service to have my work published. For a first time author it is the perfect way to start.

   I extend a huge thank you to my good friend Esther 'Edith Summer' Robbins, for the technical wrestling advice and proof reads of some early sections. She is a huge fan of the wrestling business and is training at the time of writing to enter the ring and perform. She has already built up an army of fans (dubbed the #editharmy) through her refereeing career in SWE.

   To Vince McMahon, Triple H, Shawn Michaels and everyone else at WWE – I extend my heartfelt thanks and appreciation for many great years of entertainment on television, and for creating stories and characters that have kept me glued to my screen over the past fifteen years. They may not be aware this book exists, but hopefully one day they will. Without them and their vision of great television none of this would have been possible.

   I am humbled and thankful to be a member of The Church of Jesus Christ of Latter-Day Saints. I stand grateful for the leaders and the members that have taught me much over the years and for their continued service and effort in building the Kingdom of Christ.

A special thanks go to my friends, family, work colleagues and fellow Church members, who have listened to me babble on about wrestling for the past fifteen years, and specifically over the past eighteen months about this book.

Finally, I thank the Lord and Savior Jesus Christ himself. All things are possible to those who believe.

Sharpshooters And Sermons

Foreword by "Bravehart" David Low
Pro-Wrestler 1995 – Present
Founder/Owner of SWE

I have read many books and autobiographies over the years and I often thought what I would write if someone was to ask me to do a foreword for them. Firstly, I felt honoured to be given such a chance to do this and secondly I thought I hope I don't mess this up somehow? I have known Darren Kane for almost 5 years now and he has been a good friend and a great wrestling fan to me and the other guys who wrestle in SWE.

He has always been the fan who cheered on the bad guy and boo'd the good! Except me, he has followed my career and my path in wrestling with poise and respect. I remember when he attended Hell for Lycra IX in Dewars Centre, Perth in August 2012 where I faced off against WWE Legend Tatanka for the SWE World Heavyweight championship. In my corner I had WWE Hall of Famer The "Hotrod" Rowdy Roddy Piper and in the opposite side with Tatanka was another great, WWE Hall of Famer The Million Dollar Man Ted DiBiase, There has never been and probably never will be a bigger match held in Scotland and Darren Kane was on hand to witness this legendary match unfold. Because of involvement with the hall of famers and Piper smashing Tatanka with his belt buckle I won the match and won the respect from many of my peers that day, but I was injured and Darren came up to me midway through the show and asked me how I was, he was the first to ask how I was and if everything was ok, I felt dizzy and had to sit down and Darren quickly left as he didn't want to intrude. I need to tell you that he didn't intrude and I feel grateful that he cared enough to ask me how I was doing and not just speak about the match and famous faces in it. I guess when you have a spiritual need being filled and your content in life as he is you can look past the glitz and glamour and notice if everything is ok.

I was and still am grateful for Darren that day for caring so much and helping me after what I would learn was a severe head injury (diagnosed in April 2013) This caused me 15-18 months of problems and health issues that I never thought I would recover from. In time I got better and it was because my family and friends helped me but more than that I had true wrestling fans like Darren who never stopped caring and always checked in with me to see how things were.

After an SWE show, David and Darren embrace in the ring.

I am writing the foreword from a wrestling standpoint but I am able to mention about the spiritual needs and friendship needs as I can see them in Darren and I know that he is a genuine caring person who not only attends wrestling events to be a fan but because he wants to keep in visual and touch contact with me and the others who have welcomed him in to the SWE family. Darren recently brought his family to a show and to meet me and other members of the roster and I felt so humbled that he thought enough of me to bring his family to meet me in Ardler Complex where we hold our monthly Uprising events. His family were lovely and I could see again that he was brought up in a loving environment and that his family meant the world to him.

In closing I would like to say that Darren has his priorities in order and that he believes in God, he has a first class work ethic and his family and friends are important to him. I will always remember the time Darren met me and my wife in The Toby Carvery in Perth, he made me feel like a superstar and treated me with so much respect, he then went and told his friends who were dining with him who I was and what I did. I didn't get a big head from this as I know just like Darren that everything we do is for God's Glory and that pride comes before a fall, it's good to be proud of things but it's more important to stay humble and true to yourself and everyone around you.

I think Darren is an outstanding young man who I am honoured to call my friend and probably my biggest (maybe my only) wrestling fan ever. Thank you for continued support and thank you for being you.

David

Bravehart places Darren in the 'Sharpshooter', wrestling's most infamous submission move.

Foreword by Paul Clancy
Former Stake President, Dundee Scotland

Darren is one unique individual. He is very committed to the Church and loves the Gospel deeply. He has attempted to do something very different in this book.

The prophet Nephi declared:

"I did liken all scriptures unto us, that it might be for our profit and learning."

(1st Nephi 19:23)

Indeed the teachings of the Saviour and many prophetic messages throughout scripture draw contemporary parallels through analogies, allegories and most famously parables to expound Gospel principles. The purpose of this style of writing and reasoning was to bring important principles and doctrines into a language that is familiar and contexts that are realistic to those being taught.

The symbolic form of this type of teaching helps at times to clarify understanding and the metaphors often sharpens the meaning as well as making it more memorable.

This is what Darren has attempted to do in this very interesting book.

Darren has drawn on his extensive love and knowledge of wrestling. It is easy to sense he has a passion for this form of entertainment and that it has meant much to him throughout his life. He has taken this experience and likened the Gospel to it and drawn a range of parallels that are thought provoking and novel.

We are all different and come from different backgrounds with different life experiences. Everyone makes their own journey to understanding the Gospel and the important part that Jesus Christ, the author of the Gospel , must play in the lives' of individuals who believe in Him.

These journeys to understanding, although having many areas in common, will be individual, but what is important is that final understanding reached is centred on Jesus Christ's teachings and the Gospel message and this leads in turn to a change in how we live our lives.

I have enjoyed sharing part of Darren's journey and I am sure you will find it thought provoking as well.

Paul Clancy

Prologue

"The Genesis Of Sharpshooters & Sermons"

"In the beginning" – Genesis 1:1

I grew up loving wrestling; everything about it was entertaining and exciting to me. Although I knew it was just a show, it gave me a sense of peace away from every day worries.

While watching wrestling and being honest about it, I also enjoyed learning about Religion during my high school years. However, I kept this quiet as this could have serious repercussions in playground. Religion was not the 'cool' thing to learn.

Over the years, my interest in learning of Religion dipped and grew, but my love for wrestling stayed the same. It wasn't until I came across a particular bible passage that I really wanted to know more.

A wrestler named Shawn Michaels kick started my journey towards true conversion. He had been called one of the greatest of all time, and throughout the 1990's was one of the top five wrestlers in the world. In 1998 he suffered a devastating back injury and was forced into retirement. He had a reputation throughout his career of drinking and doing drugs, and this continued after retirement. Some days he would have taken so much (to ease the pain on his back) that he would not know where he was. He married and his wife gave birth to a son. But as his son started to grow older and realised Daddy was not always well, Shawn realised the effect his behaviour was having on his family, and decided to seek help. His wife had grown up attending Church, but had fallen away in her adult years. Through her prayers and efforts, the family started to attend their local Church. Here, Shawn learnt to put in his life in the hands of Christ and overcome his addictions. Taking it all the way, he soon became a respected Bible teacher and Youth leader, with many looking to him for advice and guidance.

In August 2002, he made his comeback to competition. He entered the ring that night with a vest on, bearing the words "Philippians 4:13". After watching this amazing match, where this thought to be broken down injured man had the best match of his career (and took match of the year honours in most polls that year) I was so impressed with his performance I thought there must be something more to it than just talent. Next day at school I laid my hands on a Bible and looked up the verse on his vest. "I can do all things through Christ which strengthens me". Shawn spoke open and honestly about his conversion and beliefs over the next few years, through TV appearances, a book and a DVD set, all of which I was moved by. Not only was he a great wrestler, but a great man as well.

It was not until early 2006 that I began to think about going to Church. I had by this point finished school, was at college and planning my career. But, I felt something was amiss in my life. I felt unhappy, and needed something to guide me. I thought about Shawn when he was at his lowest, and decided perhaps attending Church would help me as it helped him. I had not thought about doing this before, as my parents were not Religious and I had no knowledge of which Church was right. None of my friends attended and no-one from my college ever mentioned church attendance. Where to begin?

I decided to pray about it. I'd never really prayed before. I had seen people pray on television, usually in times of distress or suffering. So I knelt in my room one night, and I prayed to ask God to help me find a Church. I prayed to ask for some direction in life. And then....

Nothing.

For a long time.

I carried on with life. I was by this point working in fast food, had dropped out of college and gone full time as I enjoyed having money. At this point in my life I had rarely had such a good cash flow and enjoyed spending it. I had part of a degree in computer sciences, but really unsure as to where to go next. I kept thinking there must be something more than this. I learnt there that money does not equal happiness. I did not even try to attend a Church. I knew there was so many churches' around Perth and indeed so many Religions the world over, that finding one would take time. I figured that God would send the correct one to me.

One warm summer's morning as I walked to work, the same way I went every day, I happened upon two ladies walking towards me. I was not sure what to make of them as they approached me. I read their name tags - they were Missionaries, from The Church of Jesus Christ Of Latter Day Saints.

They explained to me their 'mission' and which Church they were from. They briefly spoke of Joseph Smith - a Prophet, and of God's plan for all his Children. They left me their card and we arranged to meet a week later. I walked away, thinking this could be the answer I was looking for!

I did not research the Church at all in that week...I felt just to wait and hear their message. We met, at the Church building, along with another member as well. There, they explained the Savior's ministry, the Atonement, the great Apostasy and the Restoration by Joseph Smith. We watched a small video presentation of the Restoration. Upon seeing it and hearing their message, I remarked it was 'unbelievable yet believable". I continued to meet with them, and started to attend Church as well. A couple of weeks after our initial meeting, I found myself once again, in my room, on my knees, in the same spot as before, praying. This time I was not praying to find a Church, I was praying to find OUT if the Church Of Jesus Christ Of Latter Day Saints was true. To find out if Joseph Smith was a Prophet and the Book of Mormon truly testified of Jesus Christ. I felt this overwhelming burning that it was. A spirit touched me and gave me the hope and rejoicing I had been seeking for close to four years now. I called the missionaries, and said "let's do this".

Less than two months after our initial meeting, I was baptised and confirmed a member. I still keep in touch with those missionaries that taught me, and will forever be grateful for them and their desire to serve, teach and testify.

I had the pleasure and privilege to meet Shawn on 23rd June 2015 at a show in Glasgow. We briefly exchanged pleasantries about our faith and I explained to him it was through his example that took me on the path to Christianity, and will be forever grateful for him. I shed a couple of tears as we shook hands and parted.

He has again retired from the wrestling world, having nothing more to prove and now spends his well-earned retirement with his family and teaching at his local Church. He makes an appearance from time to time on a wrestling show, and I always smile when I see him. To me, he lived a truly good life in the wild world of pro-wrestling, and gave hope to millions of fans around the world, who continue to show their love and appreciation for him.

Almost nine years have passed since I became a member of the Church. I have not always been the best; I've had some trials, some periods of time away from the Church, and some obstacles to overcome. But it has made me stronger and made my testimony grow. Now, I feel there is nothing I can't accomplish with the will of Heavenly Father, the Atonement of Jesus Christ, and the guidance of the Holy Spirit. Shawn lives by a great motto - "All Things Are Possible To Those Who Believe".

It fits hand in hand with the scripture.

As I grew spiritually in the Church, I have found ways to relate my two passions in life – Wrestling and Religion – to help myself and others better understand the Gospel, and show just how inspiring wrestling can be when you really look at it. When a story is played out correctly, when a wrestler speaks with such passion, or when a moment just captures your heart so fully, you'll find a powerful lesson to keep forever, and relate to a gospel topic or a scripture.

This book is a collection of parables I have taught over the years and some new ones as well. Jesus Christ taught many lessons through a parable, and are still used today to not only let us learn, but to think about what we are learning and study it out in our minds.

It has given me a greater understanding of both subjects. Whether you or Religious or not, a wrestling fan or not, there will certainly be something here to make you think, laugh, cry or smile.

So, without further ado, let's get ready to rumble...

Chapter One

"This Is Going To Be Art"

The Parable Of The Wrestling Match

Doctrine & Covenants 60:13

"Thou shalt not idle away thy time, neither shalt thou bury thy talent that it may not be known."

A typical wrestling match is usually planned out in one of two ways. The more experienced and seasoned performers will generally go over the 'high spots' (the bigger and most memorable parts of the match) and weave the rest together as it progresses, depending on crowd reaction and pacing. The fact that they have been doing it so long and have the years of in ring experience, timing and crowd control makes this the best way of giving the audience an entertaining and captivating match.

Other less tenured performers will lay out their match move for move with their opponent, and generally not change much or any of it, no matter the crowd reaction (usually if the crowd loses interest they will have to do something to bring them back to attention). Even some of the most experienced performers prefer this method, think of it like ballet or a similar dance recital. The fact they have the match laid out move for move and spot to spot (and must then memorize and perhaps even rehearse with their opponent) will make the actual performance easier on them.

Ric Flair and Bret Hart were famous for agreeing the high spots beforehand, and doing the rest themselves whilst in the ring. They would pace the match and the moves based on how the crowd reacted and the story they wanted to tell ('story' being the theme of the match, such as working over a particular body part or an injury the opponent had, or the mind games they would play to catch the opponent off guard).

Ric Flair would always wrestle to damage the legs of his opponent, and along with his signature moves during the match would go for the 'figure four leg lock' to force his opponent into submission after being unable to stand. He understood how to tell the story to the audience and use the right moves at the right time. It is why he has been called one of the greatest ever.

Bret Hart was similar; he would also work on the legs before going for his signature move, the 'Sharpshooter' to force his opponent to quit. Bret loved to tell a story in his match, and would call the match as it progressed. Look for his iron man battle with Shawn Michaels at Wrestlemania 12 or his encounter with The British Bulldog at Summerslam 1992 for prime examples of excellent story telling within a match.

Diamond Dallas Page, himself a great wrestler and respected veteran, preferred to lay out his matches move for move, and would always accentuate the positives and hide the negatives of each performer. He knew the strengths and weaknesses of himself and who he'd be performing with, so would lay out the match in such a way that the crowds would only see the good.

When there is a non-wrestler involvement, such as Lawrence Taylor at Wrestlemania 11, or Floyd Mayweather at Wrestlemania 24, the match is laid out and rehearsed move for move in the months and weeks beforehand, to ensure the best match possible. Those with no experience clearly cannot call the match as it goes. It would degenerate into chaos.

Either method works, it just comes down to who is performing, their strengths, weaknesses, and routines. In short, as long as the crowds are entertained and engrossed by the match, the wrestlers have done their job and done it well.

∞

In a lot of Churches, it is the Reverend, or Vicar or Priest who will speak each Sunday from the Pulpit, and give us a Sermon or a message from the scriptures. In the LDS Church, where it is all a 'lay ministry' (the members are called to positions to lead, direct and teach); it is the members themselves who will speak from the Pulpit each Sunday to deliver a talk based on scriptural accounts and other experiences.

Much like a wrestling match, the talk can be planned in one of two ways. 'On the fly' or laid out word (move) for word (move).

Let's look at each in turn…

Perhaps those members less experienced or more nervous about public speaking will write out the talk word for word, researching their chosen subject thoroughly and putting in as many scriptures and quotes as needed. This way, they know exactly what they will say and no need to think before speaking or worry about what to say next. Let me say that there is nothing at all wrong with this; some of the best talks I have heard have been done this way. A member in my own unit who was baptised recently was very nervous about speaking in public but after much research, rewrites and checking, delivered a very powerful and captivating message on the love she has felt from other members.

More conclusive proof this is a great way of delivering a message is the LDS General Conference. The talks given by the Church leaders (the most experienced and probably least nervous of all) are assigned, prepared and written weeks in advance before delivering on the day, to allow them to be translated into other languages for members all over the world. These are some of the most uplifting and strengthening messages I have ever heard (Elder Hollands 'Safety For The Soul' October 2009, President Uchtdorf 'Lift Where You Stand October 2008, and President Monson 'Be Your Best Self' April 2009 are just some of many great examples) and coming from our beloved leaders, you know they are going to teach us and keep our attention.

Then there are those talks that are done on the fly. The person delivering it will have an idea of what they wish to speak on, has a few scriptures, quotes and experiences written down ready, but will generally deliver the message based on what they feel needs to be said and where they want the message to go. Unlike wrestling, there is no 'crowd noise' to indicate how they are coming across, but simply by looking around at their congregation (audience) they will be able to see what message they may need. My former Stake President was famous for delivering a talk this way (and in terms of verbal delivery, was up there with Ric Flair, it was always grabbing, you were able to fee a connection and involvement).

When I first joined the Church and was given speaking assignments, I would lay out every word in the talk and deliver it that way. I was very nervous, no confidence and extremely shy. I barely looked up from my paper, but was told I always gave a great message. Now, I find it easier to simply jot down a few notes and references, usually the day of the actual talk when I'm 'firing on all cylinders' and motivated. My favourite example being a talk I gave last year on being an example of Christ through love and charity, where my pointers were wrote on my ipad and the rest just came as the talk progressed. I was told after it was the best talk I have ever given, and touched a lot of people's hearts.

Of course, in Church there is a secret third option, and that is to teach and talk 'as the spirit dictates'. In truth, this should be the case in anything we do at Church. If we are faithful and let ourselves act as a mouthpiece for the spirit, we will deliver the message that the congregation needs to hear. And that is the ultimate objective of any talk in a Church setting.

In both settings, no matter how it is prepared, whether on the fly or by rigorous preparation and rehearsal, the goal is very much the same - To entertain and captivate the audience (Wrestling), and to teach and testify to the congregation (Religion).

The circumstances for preparation vary depending on the person, the setting, or the audience to deliver too. It's what makes it all so interesting, you just never know what you're going to get.

∞

This chapter is dedicated to Arthur 'Art' Jones of Logan, Utah. His style of teaching and speaking has kept me engrossed in my spiritual education, and formed a great friendship because of it.

Chapter Two

"You're Learning From The Best!"

The Parable Of The Teacher

Exodus 18:20

"And thou shalt teach them ordinances and laws, and shalt show them the way wherin they must walk, and the work that they must do."

In this book, Paul Heyman is a name you will hear a few times. To those familiar with him, he needs no introduction. To those with little or no understanding of wrestling, allow me to explain.

Paul has worked in the wrestling business for almost thirty years. Most famously (and successfully) working as a manager, he has also been placed on commentary, and served as the owner and booker of Extreme Championship Wrestling until its demise in 2001. Long been called the best talker in the business, he has carved out a career that few non-wrestlers could dream of. Managing many world champions (including Brock Lesnar) and promoting some of the most exciting shows of the late 90's, he is respected and admired by the hardcore fans of wrestling. When he speaks, people listen. He, more than perhaps any other manager in history, knows how to put his message over in such a way you that you feel you have to buy the next show or support his client.

But how did he become so knowledgeable and develop himself to where he is today? How did this fat little Jewish kid from New York become the advocate of and the man behind Brock Lesnar, his most successful client, and lead an entire wrestling company from small sideshow to worldwide phenomenon?

Well, just like most things in life (and in Church), he went to find the best and learn from them.

While employed as a photographer for wrestling shows, at age just 17, he would get his way backstage. Being the biggest wrestling fan on the planet and taking photos wasn't enough for him, he wanted to know it all. He had aspirations to do anything and everything he wanted. So one day at a show, he decided to enter a production (planning and development) meeting, run by Dusty Rhodes, who was in charge at the time.

Dusty is widely regarded as one of the greatest wrestlers in history, a flamboyant and emotional character in the 80's before semi-retiring and becoming a booker and writer into the 90's. Having a thick southern accent and hailing from Texas, he was one of a kind, and had such a high and respected knowledge of the business (Dusty sadly passed away in June 2015).

The story and legend goes, that Paul sat in the back row of the production meeting and Dusty walked in. He looked around and saw this kid that he had not met before (Paul), and asked to speak with him outside. Upon seeing him up close, he realised he was the photographer from New York and at the show that night to take pictures. He asked him what on earth he was doing in the production meeting, being a closed door meeting and invite only; it was not his place to be there! Paul, as confident and smooth as the character he has played on TV for so many years, shrugged his shoulders and said "Well sir, I'm learning from you!" There was then a long pause, where Paul in his mind thought he was about to be sent home, blacklisted and his career over at just 17 years old. But Dusty, just like Paul, as cool and hyped up as the character he played on TV, says "Well kid you're learning from the best, because I'm the American Dream Dusty Rhodes and I am a super genius, now you get back in there and you keep taking notes!".

  What Paul did there was brilliant; he identified what he wanted to learn and who was the best to learn from, and did everything he needed to do in order to accomplish that goal. From there he was able to soak up the knowledge and experience of Dusty and many others, becoming a manager in WCW, a commentator, and owner/booker of ECW. After the demise of ECW (which we'll touch on elsewhere in the book) he joined the WWF/E, where he rose to even greater heights, managing many of the top stars of the new millennium. All from that one small seemingly insignificant encounter backstage, he went from the master student to the master teacher. Now, the young stars of tomorrow go to him for advice, and he is always ready to give a colourful and entertaining story from his long and prosperous career. Just watch his DVD for many brilliant examples. He truly exemplifies the correct way to learn and then teach.

∞

In Religious terms, please do not for one second think I'm suggesting for you to invite yourself to any Church meeting you like. While most meetings are public and open to anyone, member or non-member, those leadership meetings are Sacred and may be of a personal nature.

Any Church is filled with many great leaders and teachers. In LDS, they are called of God to lead and teach us correct principles and doctrine. Chances are if you attend a Sacrament (Worship) meeting you'll hear some great teachings, as outlined in the previous chapter. If you want to learn in the Church, and most of us do, we just do what Paul Heyman did, we identify what we want to learn and find the person who teaches it best.

Perhaps there is no greater man to learn from than the master teacher himself, Jesus Christ. There are many teachings to be found in the New Testament of the Bible.

One of my favourite teachings comes from Luke 15, in the New Testament. Here, Jesus sits amongst the sinners and begins to teach them the parables of lost sons and daughters. While the first two stories concern finding one in one hundred (the lost sheep) and one in ten (the silver coin), the third and final story concerns finding one in one – the prodigal son (prodigal meaning wasteful). The son asks his Father for his share of an inheritance, to go and do as he pleases. Throughout the story, he loses his fortune through squandering and selfishness, thereby losing everything his Father had worked so hard for. A famine comes into the land, and he is forced to sell himself into slavery to survive. Not only a detestable job, but it becomes ironic that the jobs he would not do for his own Father he is now tasked with by a stranger. He discovered that once his wealth had gone, his friends disappeared as well. Realizing this, he decides to return home. On the surface it may seem he was motivated by hunger and unhappiness, but a more thorough study shows he has seen the error of his ways, and will return as a servant to his father, to repent of his previous actions and repay that which his father gave him.

In teaching this parable, Jesus shows to us that we all may rebel and leave our Heavenly Father for a time, but through the ways of the world we can be shown the error of our ways and return to him. We will become aware of the temporary happiness from worldly possessions and the eternal happiness that can be obtained from God. The story goes on to show that his Father may have had knowledge of his son's trials, probably through letters home or even that connection which a parent and child always feel, and that the Father ventured out to look for and save his long lost son. When he returned, they embraced and all was forgiven, for he knew his Son had learned a valuable lesson. It is the same for us; God will wait and even attempt to look for us, for he wants us to return. Not only did the Son return and was willing to repay what he owed, but he was forgiven and welcomed back as a Son. The same applies to us today, we have a merciful God, and provided we repent of our sins, we are welcomed back to full fellowship.

A master teacher, Jesus would make his followers think about his lessons, to allow them to become spiritually enlightened and to understand, from a worldly point of view, the principles of his Gospel. This is just one of the many teachings from his earthly ministry, a multitude of them set in parables. Just like this book, a parable allows the teacher to compare two different stories to bring out one point. It often allows the reader more scope to understand.

For anyone pursuing a Religious education, Jesus Christ is the ultimate teacher; the best to learn from, for it is his Gospel. There are many others in Church who can and will teach us the correct principles as set in the scriptures, through their own methods.

The Prophet and Apostles of the LDS Church are truly wonderful teachers, who spend their daily lives setting the example that Jesus lived, and teaching as he taught, for that is their duty. At local level in our own congregations, we may have identified someone there who sets the best example and can learn from. They do not have to be the most knowledgeable on scripture references, the most experienced and tenured member of the Church, or even the most confident. But just like Paul and Dusty, if we find that special someone that we feel we can closely learn and study from, and feel a connection that represents a mentor/student relationship, then we are set to learn from our own personal best.

Just remember to bring a notepad and pen, you're going to need it.

∞

This chapter is dedicated to John Ferrans of Fife, Scotland. A great mentor, teacher and friend, who has never once left my side.

Authors Note
I invite you to watch "Because Of Him" on the YouTube website, for a fascinating montage about Jesus Christ's role as a teacher and leader.

Chapter Three

"Try Not To Go Over The Top!"

The Parable Of The Royal Rumble Match

Elder Holland - 'We Are All Enlisted' (October 2011 General Conference)

"In almost all athletic contests of which I know, there are lines drawn on the floor or the field within which every participant must stay in order to compete. Well, the Lord has drawn lines of worthiness for those called to labour with Him in this work."

    The Royal Rumble match, a tradition held each January by the WWE, is one of the most exciting and unpredictable matches you'll see each year. Not only that, but the winner is granted a Championship match at Wrestlemania, the biggest wrestling event of the year.
    The rules are simple to follow - 30 men compete, each entering at two minute intervals. You are eliminated by being thrown over the top rope, with both feet touching the floor. The last wrestler remaining earns the title shot at Wrestlemania. Anything goes in the match, so you do everything that you can to win.

I remember teaching this parable in a Priesthood meeting at Church one Sunday. It was a lesson on staying within our spiritual boundaries to be safe and draw closer to the Lord. I decided to use wrestling to illustrate my point.

Take the 1995 edition of the match. Here, Shawn Michaels entered number one, with the British Bulldog entering number two. Both these wrestlers are highly rated performers, and very dedicated to their craft. Fans watching knew to expect a show stealing performance from both, and likely see one of them win.

Shawn throughout the match could be seen clinging to the bottom rope, staying in the middle of the ring, and playing defence. In his mind, playing defence was his best offence. He knew in order to win he must avoid being near that top rope at all costs. After a gruelling match, it came back down to how it started, Shawn Michaels vs British Bulldog. The extremely talented and athletic Michaels was caught off guard and thrown over the top rope, but was able to hold on and not let his feet touch the ground. As Bulldog went to celebrate, thinking he had won, Shawn flipped himself back over the top rope and knocked Bulldog off the turnbuckle and down to the mats. Your winner of the 1995 Royal Rumble, the Heartbreak Kid himself, Shawn Michaels. He later went on to wrestle and defeat Bret Hart in the famous iron man match at Wrestlemania, winning the World championship for the first time, and in his own words, fulfilling a boyhood dream.

Look closer at what Shawn did, by staying as far away from the top rope as much as he could, he was able to survive and win the match. He knew his boundaries; he knew his line of safety. It's a simple formula which earned him victory.

∞

  So how does this wrestling match help us understand better the Principles of Christ's gospel? The quote from Elder Holland at the start of this chapter gives a clue. The Lord gives us boundaries and draws lines around them to signify how far we can reasonably be while still being 'safe'.
  We can think of our own lives as our own personal wrestling ring, with all the good and bad things of this world in it, which we fight each day to either accept or reject. Picture in the centre of this ring, standing completely perfect and bright, is Jesus Christ. The closer you are to him, i.e. away from the edge of the ring or that top rope, the safer you are, for in the hands of Jesus Christ we are safe. Think of those ropes as our boundaries, perhaps call them the scriptures or records of the commandments that God has set for us (they bring us knowledge of our 'spiritual' safe boundaries). Now think about outside the ring, where in the Royal Rumble itself is the end zone, once you are out here you are eliminated and can kiss goodbye to your Wrestlemania main event title shot. Outside the ring are all of the things that God, Christ and the scriptures warn us against. The things that are outside our boundaries and will do spiritual and physical harm to us. Those are the things we want to fight so hard to stay away from.

Finally, picture at the top of the entrance ramp away from the ring, standing looking and surveying your life, how you live it, and your strengths and weaknesses, Satan himself. He is the one who will do all he can to draw you over the top rope and away from the boundaries that have been set for you. Once away from Christ and past your scriptures, and drawing closer to him, you've lost your own personal 'Royal Rumble Match'.

Just like any wrestler wanting to win the Rumble, you have to find in your own life a way to win. If you're on the Lord's side you have to fight tooth and nail to stay close to him and battle your way through your adversaries, and stay clear of going over the top rope and joining Satan himself. Do as Shawn did, use defence to overcome these things - i.e. studying the scriptures, attending Church, living the Commandments. We are promised if we do so, Satan will not get to us, we will attain victory and go on to Wrestlemania (Heaven). And just like Shawn's desire to win the title, it will be perfect in every way.

I should point out here that even when we are spiritually thrown over the top rope into Satan's grasp, unlike the rumble where it is 'game over', there is another way to come back to Christ. (In wrestling, this option would be called 'money in the bank'). That is the joy of repentance. Even when Satan gets the better of us, when we are away from Christ and alone from God, there is always a way back. By sincerely repenting of what we did wrong, by showing a desire to commit fully to the Gospel and by coming to appreciate the Atonement fully, we can get back in that ring and continue to fight against the evils, and make that 'Wrestlemania' dream come true. We'll look at repentance deeper in an upcoming chapter.

∞

This chapter is dedicated to Shawn Michaels himself.
Through his example and skills, this book and maybe the life I live now would not have been possible.

Chapter Four

"Remember The Moments"

The Parable Of The Missionaries

Alma 29:10

"And behold, when I see many of my brethren truly penitent, and coming to the Lord their God, then is my soul filled with joy!"

Mick Foley, now there's a guy that no-one, maybe even himself, thought could ever make it in the wrestling business. He didn't have the look, the body or the technical skill to be a wrestler they said, and should maybe look at another venture for his life.

How wrong they were. While Mick was not the typical 'cut-out' of a wrestler, everything he did and the timing of it was perfect and had the crowd in the palm of his hand. His hardcore matches and battles with the likes of The Rock, Terry Funk, Steve Austin, Triple H in his prime years, and then Randy Orton, Edge and Ric Flair in his later years are the stuff of legend. He was the ultimate 'hardcore' wrestler and a unique entertainer. Check out the film 'Beyond The Mat' for a glimpse of just what he was willing to put his body (and his family) through just to make you feel that you got your money's worth.

Much has been written about Mick's career, by himself and others. So I've no need to explain more here. I want to focus on two particular speeches he delivered in 2012 and 2013, respectively. He has a talent as well on the microphone, engaging the fans in ways few could only dream of, he's that good. I had the pleasure of meeting him and attending a live stand up show a few years back, where my friend remarked he's just as good now as he was in his prime. He returned to the WWE in 2011 as an ambassador and to help the next generation of stars become legends. The keyword there is legends.

One night he stood opposite a fine wrester by the name of CM Punk. Then in the middle of long run as a bad guy (a 'heel') and spending a year as the WWE Champion – a long time in the modern era – he would state every week how many days he had been champion. He rarely defended it, he simply liked to spout the numbers.

Months later, Mick again stood opposite another wrestler, a young hungry and vicious competitor by the name of Ryback, who the week before had attacked everybody's favourite and all around good guy, John Cena, thereby beginning a run as a heel. He explained why he attacked John, left him laying, and didn't help him when a group of three performers named 'The Shield' then attacked him further. He listed the number of times that he had been attacked by The Shield, the number of times John took the spotlight over him and the number of times John had been champion and not him. He, like CM Punk, was spouting numbers.

Cue Mick Foley for an impassioned wakeup call speech to them!

To Punk, after listening to him spout how many more days he'd been champion, Mick said '29', '29' cumulative days as champion in his three reigns combined. And after all those years, nobody cares. People just remember he was the Champion, and the matches, and the moments he provided in that time! He further explained Punks methods of retaining his championship were slightly controversial and maybe even a little sneaky. When people think of Mick's reigns, he said, they think of him doing it with heart, and guts, and pride. He finally asked Punk, and this is the best part, "Do you wanna be a legend, or do you wanna be a statistic?" He explained, passionately, that it is the moments that define us, that define our legacy, that will define Punks career and all the others. What they do every night, what they say, the matches they have, that is how they are remembered. And they do it for the fans that love and support them. He recognised that Punk had all the talent in the world, and encouraged him to define his legacy with moments, not numbers.

To Ryback, he rebuked him aswell for 'spouting statistics and charting graphs'. He explained when he went down in a fight, he'd work through the pain, come back up and keep fighting. He did the best he could, and on three separate occasions the best he could led him to be the champion. He heartedly explained to Ryback and everyone watching, that it's not about the numbers or the statistics, it's about doing your best, your absolute best, giving everything you have to what you are fighting for, and one day, it will lead to that prize of the Championship.

∞

The LDS church is a missionary church. Men and woman of all ages serve all over the world to proclaim the Gospel, share messages of Jesus Christ and invite others to follow him. Many other Religions the world over have similar works, on a large and small scale. Through Church leaders at all levels, the work is highly organised, efficient and a representation of the importance missionary work is to this Church and to the people it aims to teach.

Many missionaries however may love to boast about 'how many people they baptised on their mission' or 'how many people we taught this week' or even 'we've set a goal to baptise X number of people this month'. Now I'll state first of all there that is nothing wrong with much of this. The work is efficient and organised because of the number of goals set, goals achieved, and reports of those taught and numbers sent to leaders every single day. How would we know the Church is growing membership wise if nothing was reported?

However, it goes back to what Mick said, on a number of things. Firstly, missionaries are going to get a lot of rejection. They will knock doors, speak to people, teach people, give service to people and much more, and yet despite their message and kindness, will be told not to come back. At times, doors will be slammed on them, teachings will hailed as false and kind words will be thrown back at them. Here we can learn a parable about what Mick said. In his career he was beaten up, knocked down and in pain nearly all the time, yet he continued to get up and fight. To him, losing a match or being beaten up just fuelled him more to keep going. He did the best he could. And he was victorious. When a missionary becomes disheartened after someone rejects the message of Christ, do they pack their bags and go home? Of course not, they continue to keep doing the work, they fight to keep the cause alive, and they give it their all. That, is all the Lord asks, we give all we can. And the rewards, or blessings, will come in time.

  Another teaching we can learn is to be united. Mick spoke about Ryback leaving John Cena alone to fend for himself against a group out to destroy him. They were not united together, they had their own agendas and out for themselves. But that's just the nature of wrestling sometimes. Missionaries in the church are instructed to be united together (they serve in companionships of two or sometimes three, think of it as a tag team in wrestling. They even wear the same outfits, like the Dudley boys or the Shield). Any issues or problems they have should be worked out promptly and as directed by the spirit. If they are not working alongside each other, then they will surely not work well to speak to others about their work. It also shows you never leave your team on their own, you are together until that final whistle or bell or whatever ends it that match.

Ryback left Cena on his own, to be destroyed by the opposing side. If a missionary, or any church member, left their team mate to fend for themselves in such a setting that Cena was, they would surely succumb as well. Missionaries teach and testify together, not separately. They are stronger together, on the Lord's team.

Finally, my favourite teaching from here is the statistics. As I said, statistics play a highly important role in the monitoring of Church activity. But, the absolute most important thing to remember is a person, a soul on this earth is not, never has been and never will be, just a statistic. They are not a name on a bit of paper or a number to report back for a missionary to their leader. They are a human being who wants to hear a message from Jesus Christ, a person with a soul just waiting to be saved, a child of God – who wants to come back to him.

Nobody that a missionary encounters on their mission is a number to record, a name on a bit of paper, or a tick in a box. They are a soul, different from anyone and everyone else, and the way they are taught could be highly different from the person next to them.

When teaching anyone, a missionary (or member) should remember that this person is here to learn, grow and be saved. Make them a 'legend', someone who will be baptised and live forever. After they depart this mortal earth their name will live on in the books of history and people speak highly of them.

Missionaries will return home and tell family and friends how many baptisms they had, but what people really want to hear, are the stories, the moments that defined them in their field. I like a missionary that has stories to tell and moments to share. It might even make a great book.

It goes for members and missionaries alike, do they want to be a legend, or a statistic? Make some great moments and define your legacy that way. Then, you will have a story to tell. Just ask Mick Foley.

∞

This chapter is dedicated to the three original missionaries that taught me – Sister Hannah Macfarlane, Sister Ashley Stoker and Sister Anne Wellington. Thank you for seeing me as a soul to be saved, and for the great moments and memories we've shared over the years.

Meeting Mick Foley at the Fringe Festival, Edinburgh – August 2012

Chapter Five

"Prelude To Victory"

The Parable Of The Music

Doctrine and Covenants 25:12

"My soul delighteth in the song of the heart; yea, the song of the righteous is a prayer unto me, and it shall be answered with a blessing upon their heads"

   A wrestler's entrance music has to give the perfect setup. Much like a TV show theme or soundtrack to a movie, the music sets the tone of the wrestler it is associated with. When I think of the film 'Mary Poppins', each song showcased moved the plot long, and without that music the film would not have had the same impact that it had then and the legacy that it has today.
   Every wrestler is a character in a story, where their issues and disputes are resolved via beating each other up in the ring. We, as the audience, want to connect with them and understand why they are fighting, what each character stands for and what they think about. When they are about to enter the arena, their entrance music is played. Before we even see them, chances are we'll hear the music and know who is arriving. The music is synonymous with them,

meaning only associated with them and for them. It is a huge part of their act, and should somehow symbolize their character.

The first well known wrestler to use music in their entrance was Hulk Hogan. His 'Real American' theme was catchy, cool and showcased exactly what he stood for. He was (and still is) the icon of American wrestling, and would fight on behalf of the fans. He spent his first WWF run as the good guy than fans loved to cheer, and the music certainly helped to gain popularity.

When The Undertaker first arrived, he would use a sombre and eerie funeral march when entering, signifying his gimmick of being an old style western Undertaker and could not be hurt – because he was already dead. This, in the story, would be used to get inside his opponents head and scare them before the match even started. Today he still uses a similar tune, almost 25 years after debuting. And still, it sends shivers down fans and wrestlers spine's, it has that good an effect.

Triple H, when he became 'The Game', the wrestler who everyone else was to measure up to, as he claimed to be 'that damn good', had the band Motorhead record music with words to that effect. Based on his talents and combined with that music, fans could genuinely believe he was the best. Being a big Triple H fan myself, I echo this. In his prime he was the absolute best.

And finally, Ric Flair for most of his career use the music "Dawn" taken from "Also Sprach Zarathustra" by Richard Strauss. You may not recognise that, but put it into YouTube and give it a listen, and you'll know it. It symbolizes everything Ric was about – respect, admiration, attention, magnificence, and star power. When you heard it, you knew you were about to be in the presence of wrestling royalty. It signified a time to stand and show respect, for in most fans' eyes he is the greatest of all time. I had the fortune to attend a meet and greet with Ric Flair this year, and when he was making his way into the room, the music played. Just like old times, everyone stood in respect and admiration.

The music gives us more information about the character and what they stand for. It's all about character development in wrestling. If we don't understand anything or know anything about who we are watching, why would we bother paying to see it? The music gives us the setup to get excited to see them and start that connection. When CM Punk used 'Cult Of Personality' as his entrance, fans would be in anticipation of what he was about to say or do. His character was that of an outsider and not afraid to speak his mind or deviate from the norm. The music was the most perfect way to set his impending arrival up, you just knew it was a special moment. It prepared us for what lay ahead, and that's how you keep the show flowing – preparation for what is next.

∞

Go to any Church, LDS or not, and you'll hear music. Go to any church and they'll probably have a church choir. All will have people that can sing, or think they can sing. Churches and music are synonymous with each other, people worship through songs and singing, just as the scripture at the start of this chapter suggests.

Just like in wrestling, it's all part of preparation. Prelude music is played before most worship meetings, to allow the congregation to maintain reverence and reflection on why they are at Church. It prepares them for the service ahead, to get in the right frame of mind. Without it, people could just be sitting talking away and catching up with friends, forgetting the real reason they are there. Like Ric's entrance music, the prelude music commands the respect of the people in attendance.

The Sacrament, also known as communion and many other names, is the main and most dignified part of any worship service. Here, bread is broken by members of the Priesthood to remember the Atonement of Jesus Christ. But never done in silence, at least not in the LDS church, it is done while the congregation sing a hymn together, one that focuses on Jesus Christ himself. We prepare to remember his sacrifice by singing praise to Him. It is an integral part of the ordinance, helping to focus in our minds.

Hymns are sung in almost every meeting and class the LDS church has, they allow us to focus our minds on our roles ("I am a child of God"), our leaders ("Praise to the Man") and to Jesus Christ himself ("How Great Thou Art"). And I can't write about music without mentioning the world famous 'Mormon Tabernacle Choir', who have sung for the President of the USA many times, opened the Winter Olympics in Utah, and sing at every General Conference, to name a few of their illustrious performances. I love the music of the Church. It inspires me, motivates me, teaches me and most of all draws my attention to that which I should be focused on.

Just like in wrestling, it's the perfect setup.

∞

This chapter is dedicated to all the church members I know that love to share their testimony via song, you always uplift anyone in your presence.

Meeting 'Nature Boy' Ric Flair, taken May 2015 – Edinburgh, Scotland.

Chapter Six

The Omega Line-up

So we've covered a few chapters now and learnt some of the great parables that wrestling and Religion can bring. I wanted to add a chapter about the times they have crossed over. Yes, wrestling is a business and will do (almost) anything to sell tickets and make money. Sometimes, it involved exploiting Religion.

Apart from Shawn Michaels, who is featured in this book a lot, Religious characters in wrestling are generally portrayed as the bad guys and sometimes slightly insane. Only Shawn, based on his fame and respect among peers has been allowed to represent his views respectfully. But alas, wrestling is just a show, we are not meant to take it as real life. Here, we looked at some characters in wrestling who had Religious overtones or gimmicks. Some worked, and some didn't.

Brother Love
The alter ego of Bruce Pritchard, debuted at a time when ministers were all over TV preaching sermons and going over the top with them. Brother Love was just that, although he claimed to be preaching the 'Word Of Love' and not the 'Word Of God'. One segment showed him 'healing' a man who was blind and deaf, in the manner of Jesus Christ. After several complaints, the character was written out and used

sporadically since. Behind the scenes, Bruce is a talented writer and consultant.

Friar Ferguson
Played by the late Mike Shaw, this was a monk who wrestled and got madder each time seen on TV. It wasn't long before the Catholic Church in New York sent complaints, and the character was dropped.

Reverend D-Von
Oh testify! D-von Dudley was split from his storyline brother Bubba Ray, and given a new gimmick as a Reverend and Preacher. In real life, D-von's parents were Christian ministers, so he knew how to play the role with effect. He would arrive at the ring with choir music, perform the sign of the crucifixion, and encourage the audience to repent of their sins. He even had a Deacon, (the future Batista) accompany him to the ring with a box, for fans to donate money to his cause. In real life, the money collected was donated to his parent's Church. After he and his Deacon went their separate ways, and feeling the character had run as far as it could, D-von dropped the Preacher gimmick and teamed up with Bubba once again.

Mordecai
A series of videos hyped his debut, in which a man dressed in white, and hair and beard dyed blonde as a sign of purity, claimed he was on a mission to rid the world of sin and evil. The name comes from a character in the Book Of Esther, in

the Old Testament. He debuted in the ring and defeated a number of opening match wrestlers, before setting his sights on The Undertaker. It would have been a great feud with intense promos and special effects galore, but Mordecai was sent away for further in-ring training as management did not feel he had enough experience. Maybe one day he will return.

Kevin Sullivan
In the late 1970's and early 80's, Kevin performed a devil worship gimmick, along with a group of other wrestlers. His most famous 'follower' was the 'The Fallen Angel', who in real life he was married too.

Muhammed Hassan and Daivari
In 2005, the WWE brought the offence to Muslims everywhere when Muhammed Hassan, an Arab-American, wanted relief and peace from prejudice that the Muslim community were facing. He would raise his hands to Allah in prayer. His manager, Daivari would then repeat his words in Persian language. After a few months of mildly impressive performances against the likes of Hulk Hogan, Shawn Michaels and John Cena, he was matched against The Undertaker. It went from bad to worse in one night when Daivari was offered as a 'Sacrifice' to Undertaker, who was beaten quickly. Then, in a controversial moment, Hassan raised his hands to the sky before a group of masked men ran out to attack Undertaker, using piano wire to choke him out. Daivari was then carried out above their heads.

Hassan would never appear on TV again. His last appearance was on PPV at The Great American Bash, where Undertaker power bombed Hassan through the stage. Hassan, real name Mark Copani now teaches High School social studies.

The Undertaker
His character has gone through many changes over the years, adding layers and dimensions. It was in 1999 that he followed on from Kevin Sullivan's gimmick and took it one step further. The Undertaker led a 'ministry' and was leading a crusade to take over the WWF. He abducted wrestlers and made them offer a blood sacrifice, in turn gaining membership to his 'cult'. It was later revealed to be Vince McMahon as the 'higher power' that Undertaker kept speaking of (most thought it was Satan himself). The angle finished a few months later when Vince left TV as a character and Undertaker was forced out with an injury. He returned as the more human Undertaker, riding a motorbike, a year later.

Bray Wyatt and The Wyatt Family
This one is not strictly a Religious character, more a cult leader with a following. Debuting in 2013, Bray had a rough start only to develop into an all-round great talent and character. Surrounded by his two 'followers' – Luke Harper and Erik Rowan, Bray cast fear into the entire WWE Universe with his creepy and mesmerising speeches about love, following his path and destroying his opponents. He would constantly reference a 'Sister Abigail', believed to be a nun

that raised him only to die suddenly, causing him to morph into the man we see before us today. One of his greatest moments came during a feud with John Cena. In a segment on Raw, Bray played mind games by having a children's choir sing "He's got the whole world in his hands" as John stood in the ring, visibly shaken and scared by what he saw before him. As Bray and his followers joined them, the children surrounded the ring while Bray sang with them. The lights went to black, returning to find the children now wearing sheep masks, the same one Erik would wear to signify his dedication to Bray. As John stood, defeated and upset, Bray laughed sadistically into the microphone, having gotten inside the head of Cena. His entrance music alone did that.

Chapter Seven

"Do It My Way!"

The Parable Of The Great Leader

John 14:6

"Jesus saith unto him, I am the way, the truth, and the life: no man cometh unto the Father, but by me."

In both wrestling and in Church, you'll always get some people who think that they know better than those in charge, and will have their own ideas about what is 'best for business' or 'best for the congregation'. Both organizations have selected and well trained leadership, who understand what is required of them and the knowledge to direct and administer correctly that which is put upon them.

Triple H is a great and masterful wrestler who has now semi-retired from the ring and taken on a more executive role in the WWE, both behind the scenes and in the story. He spoke recently about the correct way to run what is fast becoming his wrestling company on a podcast with another legend – Stone Cold Steve Austin. Triple H has spearheaded the initiative over the past few years to introduce younger and fresher talent into the shows each week. He understands that the business evolves and the stars of the past ten years will not be around forever. He calls it the 'NXT Generation'. The talent of tomorrow is evolving today, the future is now, he proclaims.

He debated in the interview with Steve, about the ways of learning in the wrestling business. Some go to a school, learn and then wrestle all over the world in different settings and with different rules governing how they perform, and what they can and cannot do. Some go to a school, learn and then simply wrestle on a part time basis, seeing it as more a hobby than a career. And recently, some after finishing wrestling school make it a goal to find a way into the WWE, through the NXT division. It is here that receive the absolute best training possible, guided by many great wrestlers of the past.

Everything in that division is done Triple H's way. It is his brainchild, his project, his vision. A man that has seen and done it all. He is one of the greatest of all time, knows exactly what is required to make it in the wrestling business. He was nicknamed 'The Game' in his prime years, based on being that good and smart like a computer. He compared (and here we have a parable within a parable) NXT to an American football league. An athlete can play on one team for many years, running the plays that the coach has devised and performing the way he has been told to, and the way he has grown accustomed to. That might work in that team, and that's fine. But say he then transfers to a new team, with a new coach, new tactics and new plays. And the player, perhaps thinking he knows best or maybe a desire to prove himself, decides to stick to his old ways. He ignores the coaches advice and does it his way. With that, the team is not on the same page, even the same book, and the game (no pun intended to Triple H) is lost. If the player came in as a dry sponge, ready to soak up all the water – the knowledge and guidance and rules – that the coach and the rest of the team have learned, they have every chance of winning.

Going back to NXT, wrestlers from all over the world are coming in and hoping to make it into WWE via the developmental league. They all have different backgrounds, styles, rules and rituals. Wrestling styles differ in every country and company, some focusing on high flying (Mexico), some on holds and mat wrestling (Japan), some on blood and violence (backyard promotions and East Coast organizations for a time) and some focus on the overall package (WWE & TNA). Here, they are taught to bring all they have learnt, and mould themselves into the WWE style that Triple H has set out. It is the perfect template, where every detail is planned out and executed after much training and practice. The goal is to mould each performer to be comfortable and ready on the main stage, that being the weekly WWE television shows, PPV and if they really develop their talent, Wrestlemania. They are running Triple H's playbook, doing it his way. He understands the correct ways so well, that he can be trusted to guide the careers of every single performer coming in.

The beauty of NXT is that it is a learning program, mistakes will happen and things will go wrong. The fact it is attended and watched by a lesser audience, and aware of the experience levels of who they are seeing makes the league a fantastic place to hone their skills and work on their act. Triple H explains if they make a mistake, they'll learn from it and move on. It is what the business needs to evolve, it is what the wrestlers themselves need to learn, and perhaps even the fans need it to appreciate just how much each wrestler does to develop and be ready to perform in front of the crowds.

It is really all about trust, willpower and respect. Triple H has the way, and if they want to be successful, it has to be followed.

∞

In Church, just as in NXT, there is only one way, and that is The Lord's way. It is something I have thought about a lot over my years in the LDS church. It may be run on earth by men – a Prophet or a Stake President or a Branch President or Bishop. But they are all called and chosen by God, to be his mouthpiece and representative here on Earth. Any decision they make is done through prayer and study, not by their own ideas or opinions, education or professional lives.

Most people have the right attitude, but I have seen in my time some who want to run and direct the Church's affairs in the way they see fit, based on their opinion and efforts in their lives. I am not intending to offend or disrespect anyone in this chapter, I am simply using this to teach the parable.

Many will do it correctly; they will come to Church as a dry sponge, ready to soak up everything they hear that day. They are ready and willing to learn, humbling themselves and accepting they do not know what is best. But there are always some who might think they know better, or know enough, or are there as the benchmark for others to rise too. Those are the ones that have the most to learn. Perhaps it is not always realised and acted upon, but it can happen to us all.

Jesus Christ, as stated in the scripture above, is the way, the only way. Through him we will attain victory. By following his counsel and direction, and doing it his way, we will never be steered wrongly. Just like in wrestling and into NXT, people will come to Church from all walks of life and many times from great Religious backgrounds. They are encouraged to 'bring all the good and wonderful' with them, we are respectful of all other Religions and recognise them as great and caring places. However, they may be accustomed to abiding by the precepts that one member has set, or by the rules simply dictated at their particular place of Worship, or teaching doctrine that the more outspoken members have decided upon over time. They are going by their own playbook and own agenda. In The Church Of Jesus Christ Of Latter Day Saints, it is one set of rules and one set of doctrine, that which has been given to us from the Heavens above.

The Church is the perfect template, just like NXT it could be called a developmental ground. We are here to learn and to grow, based on the outline Jesus Christ has for us. We will make mistakes, things will go wrong in our lives, we will have trials and setbacks and feelings of hopelessness. But I can guarantee we'll have a lot of good as well. It is all preparation for our own personal journey to the main stage, to our own personal 'Wrestlemania', that is to be reunited with the Savior and to reach the glories of Heaven. Only by abiding by the correct doctrine, studying the scriptures and living the principles taught to us, can we reach that goal.

Much like the NXT wrestlers will study old footage of matches and critique themselves to improve their own matches, we must study the examples in our scriptures and look at our lives to learn how we can and will become better. Much like they cannot learn Triple H's way and then simply go out and do what they think is best in the ring, can any Church member study the life of Christ and then go away and do something contrary to it. That is not how any one person can have success. If they know what is best to attain success in either wrestling or in Church or any other walk of life, it must be followed.

We are here to do it the Lord's way, the way he sees fit for us. He has set out the playbook for us, to guide and direct the correct way. Only by humbling ourselves and accepting him as our Master and leader can make it to 'Wrestlemania'.

∞

This chapter is dedicated to Daryl Watson of Fife, Scotland. The first Stake President I ever knew and a great one at that. A truly remarkable leader, a teacher and friend.

Chapter Eight

"Bret Came Home, He's Fine. They Murdered The Hitman"

The Parable Of Betrayal

Psalms 43:1

"Plead my cause against an ungodly nation: O deliver me from the deceitful and unjust man."

    This is perhaps the most talked about incident in the history of professional wrestling – a tale of loyalty, deceit, betrayal and redemption. What follows is an account of a very real life situation that ultimately led to one moment on television, changing the business forever. The reading of it however cannot do it full justice, and I recommend watching the documentary 'Wrestling With Shadows' for a greater understanding.
    The year is 1997. Bret Hart is the biggest star in the WWF and reigning World Heavyweight Champion. The WWF is losing the popularity and ratings war to its direct competition on another channel – World Championship Wrestling (WCW). Having been loyal to his boss Vince Mcmahon for over twelve years and doing everything asked of him, Bret had signed a twenty year contract with the WWF in 1996, guaranteeing

him great money and a prominent position for years to come. He had previously negotiated with WCW officials before ultimately resigning with WWF, out of loyalty and respect to Vince.

However, as the battle between WWF and WCW raged on, and with the WWF losing money each week, Vince decided he had to cut costs. One of his first cuts was to be the contract of Bret Hart. Vince informed Bret that he could no longer afford to pay his salary, and should reopen negotiations with WCW straight away. Although sad to be losing his top star, Vince felt he could not pay Bret what he deserved. After successfully signing with WCW and agreeing a start date of December 1997, there was the small matter of to whom, how and when Bret would drop his coveted WWF Championship before leaving.

At the time, the proud Canadian wrestler was feuding with Shawn Michaels, both on television and backstage in real life scenarios. Jealousy and ego would often get the better of the two, leading to many real life fights and arguments. Back then, Shawn admits himself he was not an easy guy to work with and to be around. There was a PPV coming up in November, the Survivor Series. It was to be held in Montreal, Canada. Bret was in a situation at the time where he played the bad guy on television, but in Canada he was still seen as a hero and cheered whenever he went there. "Everybody needs a hero" he claimed, and to Canadians he was their favourite hero. Bret had it written into his contract that in the event of him leaving the company, he would have 'reasonable creative control over his on screen character' for the last thirty days of his time there. Meaning, he would not do anything that he was not happy with on screen.

Vince felt the right scenario, the one that is best for business, would be for Bret to lose to Shawn, fairly, at Survivor Series and then bow out. It was then cement Shawn Michaels as the WWFs biggest star. But Bret, realising it meant losing in his home country in front of his adoring fans, vetoed the idea. He would lose to Shawn on any other night in any other place, but not in Montreal. It was then agreed that the two would wrestle at Survivor Series as planned, but the match would end when members of Bret's team (The Hart Foundation) and Shawn Michaels team (D-Generation X) would interfere, resulting in a disqualification and Bret would retain the Championship. Bret would then appear on Raw the next night forfeit the championship, say goodbye and depart for WCW. The entire conversation with Vince to plan this was taped, as Bret wore a secret microphone while filming for the above mentioned documentary.

What followed at Survivor Series was a rollercoaster of a battle between Bret and Shawn. They held nothing back and went for it all. Vince McMahon was at ringside to oversee the match. The referee Earl Hebner, a friend to both men for years, had promised Bret, on his kid's lives that he would not let anything happen to him in the ring.

But, it was not to be. Nearing the end of the match, Shawn locked Bret in the submission move known as the Sharpshooter, which was Bret's finishing move. If Bret tapped, it meant he had given up and the Championship would be awarded to Shawn. However, straight away Earl

Hebner and Vince McMahon called for the bell and declared Shawn the winner. Bret never tapped or gave up, he had been screwed over.

He looked around to see his fans were angry, he was upset, and Shawn sat beside the ropes in disbelief at what just happened. Seeing Vince, he spat on him and destroyed parts of the ringside area. In his mind, he was thinking why after years of loyalty and hard work could he screw me over like this?

Backstage, Shawn swore that he was not in on it, he had no knowledge of what would happen. It was caught on camera. Years later, after much suspicion, it came out that Shawn (and Triple H) knew beforehand that it would end that way. Bret's wife and children were backstage as well, visibly upset and hurt at the situation.

Bret was able to get into Vince's office, and punched him in the face, knocking him to the ground. It was never shown on camera. With that, Bret departed the arena with his family, his career in the WWF over and bound for WCW. While still in the ring earlier that night, he spelled out the letters 'WCW' in the air and encouraged his fans to follow him there.

The next night on Raw, Vince would explain his actions at Survivor Series. He claimed that Bret would not honour the tradition of the wrestling business, which is to 'pass the torch' to your opponent on your last night with the company and show that he is now the top star. The immortal line was uttered by Vince - "Bret screwed Bret". It was clear from Vince's message and actions that he thought Bret should have left the correct way on Montreal, to allow his wrestling

company to carry on with Shawn at the helm. He did not like Bret's way of doing it (Bret forfeiting the championship and leaving without ever losing it in a match was not the correct way of departing in his mind).
  The 'Wrestling With Shadows' documentary ends with Bret's comments in the months following Survivor Series;

"It's almost fitting end to the Hitman character, he never sold out and he never lost his integrity. Bret Hart came home, he's fine. What they did is they murdered the Hitman character"

  He was absolutely right. Bret always stood for what was right, honest and true. Even while playing the bad guy during the final part of his WWF stint (having been a good guy for most of it) he still stood for the same things. Bret came home and got on with life, though his WCW run would not be even as half as successful as his WWF career due to mismanagement and shoddy business decisions (but that's another story).
  As the years passed, Bret would continue to talk about Montreal and how Vince was wrong to do what he did. It caused a downward spiral in his life that took years to recover from. Eventually however, all wounds are healed it seems. Bret met with Vince a number of times following Owen Harts funeral in 1999 (Bret's brother, who still worked for WWF following Survivor Series and died in a terrible accident) and after nine years they buried the hatchet and worked together once again. Bret was also able to forgive

Shawn and become friends with him, now the two legends share a great respect with each other.

But, the events of Survivor Series 1997 will never truly be forgotten. It demonstrated ego, feelings of trust being destroyed, and a loyal man being incredibly hurt by someone he shared a common bond with, all to satisfy his own needs.

∞

An incredible story of betrayal and loyalty can also be found in the Bible, almost mirroring some of the events above.

When Jesus Christ led his mortal ministry, he called twelve Apostles to assist him in the great work. These men were loyal to him, just as he was loyal to them. They had a glorious few years together, and did many great works. But, Jesus knew of the plan God had set for him, and knew he would eventually find death on the cross, performing the Atonement for the entire world.

On his final night on Earth, Jesus took part in the last supper with his Apostles. He washed their feet afterwards, signifying them all as equals. He gave unto them the commandment to 'love one another, as I have loved you' (John 13:34). He also revealed to his Apostles that one of them shall betray him.

While Bret was not aware of the betrayal being set up by Vince (though he admits to having entered the match with a bad feeling), Jesus knew of his betrayer being the almighty and powerful Lord he is.

The following account is from John 13, where Jesus identifies said betrayer;

"When Jesus had thus said, he was troubled in spirit, and testified, and said, Verily, verily, I say unto you, that one of you shall betray me.
Then the disciples looked one on another, doubting of whom he spake.
Now there was leaning on Jesus' bosom one of his disciples, whom Jesus loved.
Simon Peter therefore beckoned to him, that he should ask who it should be of whom he spake.
He then lying on Jesus' breast saith unto him, Lord, who is it?
Jesus answered, He it is, to whom I shall give a sop, when I have dipped it. And when he had dipped the sop, he gave it to Judas Iscariot, the son of Simon."

It was also recorded in Matthew 26: 14-16 that Judas would be the betrayer of Jesus;

"Then one of the twelve, called Judas Iscariot, went unto the chief priests,
And said unto them, What will ye give me, and I will deliver him unto you? And they covenanted with him for thirty pieces of silver.
And from that time he sought opportunity to betray him."

The same chapter also gives a different perspective on Jesus identifying his betrayer (20-23);

"Now when the even was come, he (Jesus) sat down with the twelve.
And as they did eat, he said, Verily I say unto you, that one of you shall betray me.
And they were exceeding sorrowful, and began every one of them to say unto him, Lord, is it I?
And he answered and said, He that dippeth his hand with me in the dish, the same shall betray me."

It is interesting to see what is going on here in the exchange between Jesus and Judas, and also the other Apostles sitting around the table as well. Jesus knew exactly who his betrayer would be, yet he allowed the Apostles to question themselves by saying "Is it I?"

There was no smirking and winking at each other, claiming it could be someone else and accusing each other. These were men of God, and could only judge themselves and not others. They dared not question any of their fellow Apostles. To do so would bring disrespect to everything they had accomplished.

For those wondering, a 'sop' is a small piece of bread typically offered by the host (in this case, Jesus) to his guests (in this case, the Apostles) to go with their feast. He had offered it to all, including Judas. Perhaps this was a final test for Judas. An act of kindness from his Master, a showing of love, could he really still betray him? Could he then search his soul and realise that what he was doing was wrong and needed to stop? Whatever his decision, Jesus advised him to make it now, as recorded in John 13:27;

> "And after the sop Satan entered into him. Then said Jesus unto him, That thou doest, do quickly."

    This scripture would show that Jesus was aware of Judas and his final decision, and the time had come to act. Following this, Judas left. The remaining eleven Apostles were not aware that Judas was the betrayer, they were under the impression that he may have gone to buy more supplies for the feast, or to give what remained to the poor. He took the bag (recorded in verse 29) which is thought to have meant the funds they had, and went out into the night.
    With his betrayer (again, only known to him) gone, Jesus taught his Apostles again, instituting the Sacrament and commanding them to love one another. It would be his final lesson with them before the Crucifixion. He knew it was time to leave them, but promised he would return;

> "Ye have heard how I said unto you, I go away, and come again unto you. If ye loved me, ye would rejoice, because I said, I go unto the Father: for my Father is greater than I."

    Following his final discourse, he and the remaining Apostles made their way to Gethsemane, where they often visited together. Judas knew this, and there in the garden he awaited Jesus, with a band of Romans and other men to arrest him. Judas had betrayed his Master and handed him over for death.

So why did Judas do this? Why did a man who claimed to follow Jesus, love him and serve him then give him up for 30 pieces of silver? Did he really gain anything from it? Was it, perhaps like Vince and Bret, him trying to rule over someone else? Was it an act of spite?

There have been many theories put forward. It was prophesised in the Old Testament that someone would betray the man known that would come to be known as Jesus Christ (Psalm 41:9). There is evidence in the New Testament that suggests Judas did not see Jesus as the Savior, just a great teacher. And that he did not enjoy the same personal relationship with Jesus as the other disciples (he was listed last whenever the names of the Apostles were mentioned in the Bible). And finally, there is very little evidence of dialogue between Judas and Jesus recorded in the New Testament. Only the betrayal and a few other events are mentioned.

A theory that has been put forward is that Judas was acting out of greed and pursuit of power. He may have thought that Jesus Christ was working to rule over the nation of Israel, and could benefit in some way by acting as an Apostle. When he understood later than Jesus Christ was on earth to fulfil the Atonement, he betrayed him for whatever reward he could get and would then move onto something else, he realised he would gain no earthly power for himself.

There is no direct account I can find which demonstrates Jesus feelings towards Judas after the betrayal. Perhaps it was something that was just meant to be however, as it was prophesised in Psalms, and if Judas had not told the Romans where to find him, would Jesus have been captured and crucified, thereby performing the Atonement and allowing all mankind to be saved? Perhaps it was all part of the much bigger picture.

And whatever happened to Judas following his betrayal? Was he able to use his new found wealth to become richer? Did he gain power elsewhere that he seemed to long for and hold dear to his heart? Not quite. It is recorded in Matthew 27:3-5

"Then Judas, which had betrayed him, when he saw that he was condemned, repented himself, and brought again the thirty pieces of silver to the chief priests and elders, Saying, I have sinned in that I have betrayed the innocent blood. And they said, What is that to us? see thou to that. And he cast down the pieces of silver in the temple, and departed, and went and hanged himself."

Realising that the man he thought of as nothing more than a great teacher really was the Savior of the world, and that he had meant nothing more than thirty pieces of silver to him, the guilt poured over him. Disregarding his 'reward', he took his own life.

The story ends on a similar note to that of the hero of our wrestling tale, where Bret spoke about WWF murdering his character, but the man behind it, he came home – he's fine. The mortal Jesus Christ was killed. But the immortal and perfect son of God, he went home to his Father in Heaven and he too, was fine. He was able to carry on his work as a resurrected and immortal being.

And, happily, Bret returned home to WWE in 2010, to conclude what had started at Survivor Series almost thirteen years earlier. In the story, Bret returned to avenge the wrong that Vince McMahon had done in the past and beat him at Wrestlemania, Vince's most grand creation. The circle was complete. Bret was now at peace with his betrayer.

∞

This chapter is dedicated to my hero, Bret Hart. He represents the good in the world, battling all those who dare to deceive, betray and lie.

Chapter Nine

"You Are The Legend Makers!"

The Parable Of The Followers

Luke 9:57

"And it came to pass, that, as they went in the way, a certain man said unto him, Lord, I will follow thee whithersoever thou goest"

(Author's Note: This chapter is put together from a talk prepared for delivering in a Sacrament meeting, with some added points especially for the book.)

I can't write a wrestling book without mentioning a favourite and legendary wrestler from the olden days – The Ultimate Warrior.

Jim 'Ultimate Warrior' Hellwig was one of those wrestlers that captured the fans attention with ease. His wild promos, bursting entrance, rope shaking trademark, outstanding physique and legendary matches made him one of the centre pieces of the 1980's and beyond. Beating Hulk Hogan for the WWF title at Wrestlemania 6 stands as his most glorious moment.

After leaving the WWF and spending time in WCW, he retired from the spotlight of the wrestling world in 1998 to raise his family, enjoy the fruits of his labour and became a motivational and political speaker. Apparently on bad terms with WWF management over those years, they made peace with each other and he returned home to the now WWE in 2014.

At Wrestlemania weekend, on April 5th 2015, Ultimate Warrior was inducted into the WWE Hall Of Fame, in front of many past, present and future WWE stars, along with his wife Dana and two daughters. He would go on to say it was his proudest moment and career had come full circle.

On WWE Raw, April 7th, he came to the ring in full Warrior costume and delivered the following speech;

"No WWE talent becomes a legend on their own. Every man's heart one day beats its final beat. His lungs breathe a final breath. And if what that man did in his life makes the blood pulse through the body of others and makes them believe deeper and something larger than life then his essence, his spirit, will be immortalized. By the story tellers, by the loyalty, by the memory of those who honour him and make the running the man did live forever. (Pointing to different sections of the crowd) You, you, you, you, you, you are the legend makers of Ultimate Warrior. In the back I see many potential legends. Some of them with Warrior spirits. And you will do the same for them. You will decide if they lived with the passion and intensity. So much so that you will tell your stories and you will make them legends, as well. I am the Ultimate Warrior. You are the Ultimate Warrior fans. And the spirit of the Ultimate Warrior will run forever!"

Warrior passed away just twenty four hours later. I remember it so well. Going through an airport to fly to London I saw a message pop up on my phone, scanning briefly, I read 'Ultimate Warrior' before putting it away to check into my flight. Later, while boarding, I read it fully and was deeply saddened reading of his death, as were many the world over. It seemed so sudden and came at such a memorable and emotional time for his family and his fans. His final promo, delivered the night previously, almost feels like he gave his own eulogy, as if he knew what was about to happen. It was remarked by those who saw him up close he looked to be in pain and sweating profusely the entire weekend, but his death came as a shock to all. He leaves behind a beautiful family and a legacy which all wrestlers will aspire to and admire for years to come.

  His final words on Raw have been studied and commented on by many, discussing what it really means and the message he put across. Breaking it down, the moral is that the fans of the wrestling world decide who they will support, cheer, boo, dislike, love, hate and all the other emotions and actions that any 'hardcore' fan will show. It is them that decide who will live on through the history of time and those that did not connect with them and will simply fade away. They will write about them in books, magazines, internet blogs and so forth, their names and actions will be kept for the fans of tomorrow to read about and learn from.

  The life and career of Ultimate Warrior show this. His first major WWF run ended in the early 90's, but because of what he did in that time he was talked about with passion by many fans since then, and they longed for his return. My friend Neil would tell me stories about watching him on TV when he was young and being captivated by everything Warrior did, he was just that entertaining and good, you never knew what was coming next with him. Now, thanks to video sharing websites we can see him at his best and relive those moments.

  Warrior went on to say they are many potential 'Ultimate Warriors' in the WWE today, and they must do all they can to make that connection with the audience and 'make the blood pulse through the body of others'. Their names, legacies and moments will be talked about by fans for years after their prime, by heeding to Warriors advice.

It is chilling, when reading the words "Every man's heart one day beats its final beat, his lungs breathe a final breath". To me, and many others, he is saying you never know when your time on earth is up. He is saying to do all you can to build your legacy, to become a legend (thank you Mick Foley) and make such an impact that people will remember your moments (thank you again Mick) forever. There is absolutely no doubt that The Ultimate Warrior did this, he lived his final few days to the max.

∞

The first four Gospels of the New Testament – Matthew, Mark, Luke and John, refer to and are written specifically at the time and about the life and teachings of Jesus Christ. Scholars, Church members, professors of Religion, and Ministry leaders the world over spend their lives studying daily and learning from these four books.

The life, ministry, death and resurrection of Jesus Christ may be perhaps the best known story of our time or of any time. Indeed, almost 2000 years have passed since his mortal presence was here on Earth, and still it is examined and taught and inspiring to millions. I am not qualified enough and do not consider myself educated enough to here recount the life of Jesus Christ to you. For that I direct you to 'Jesus The Christ' by James E Talmage, a fascinating and complete journey through his life, written through intensive research and divine revelation.

However the most important books that testify of Christ are the Bible and the Book Of Mormon which stand as a witness and legacy of Jesus Christ. Each week in Church meetings all over the world, people speak from the pulpit and in classes about Him, testifying of his work and delivering a powerful message to those in attendance. Jesus Christ himself became immortal following the Atonement, and because of the scriptures, the books, the magazines, talks and videos produced over time, his life is able to be read and studied by all.

How could anyone today know of Jesus Christ if a record of his earthly Ministry and actions were not kept as it proceeded? He himself one day took his final breath, his heart beat its final beat, but his legend will live forever, through what has been written and said about him.

Let's take a look at some of the records. I would like to explain a number of events which stand out most to me. These events have been discussed in Sunday school classes around the world, both in LDS churches and any other kind of Church that accepts the New Testament as pure doctrine and scripture. It is through His actions that have been recorded that we, the people, learn and grow. If humble and willing, these actions inspire us and will encourage us to do the same, by following his example – they make the life that Jesus Christ led live forever and honour him.

The Book of John is my favourite to quote from, his writings stand out to me the most for reasons I can't quite explain, they are just simply the most powerful. So I will use some of those verses, in chronological order.

John 1:29 reads;
"John seeth Jesus coming unto him, and saith, Behold the Lamb of God, which taketh away the sin of the world".
A testament of His purpose, that through him are sins can be forgiven. Reports are written in the business world about the

purpose of multi-million pound projects and investments that are literally hundreds of pages long and detail everything, yet the greatest 'project' the world has ever seen is explained in one tiny little verse.

John 3: 16 & 17 reads;
"For God so loved the world, that he gave his only begotten Son, that whosoever believeth in him should not perish, but have everlasting life.
For God sent not his Son into the world to condemn the world; but that the world through him might be saved".
Jesus did not come here to condemn us, but to save us. That is an important part, and any follower of Christ should never feel they have authority to judge another, they are simply to be an example. Verse 16 is perhaps one of the most quoted scriptures ever, stating we will never truly perish if we believe in Christ and of Christ.

John 5:39
"Search the scriptures; for in them ye think ye have eternal life: and they are they which testify of me".
An appropriate verse for this part of the book, the storytellers write of Jesus' ministry for all to hear and read.

John 8:4-12
"They say unto him, Master, this woman was taken in adultery, in the very act.
Now Moses in the law commanded us, that such should be stoned: but what sayest thou?
This they said, tempting him, that they might have to accuse him. But Jesus stooped down, and with his finger wrote on the ground, as though he heard them not.

So when they continued asking him, he lifted up himself, and said unto them, He that is without sin among you, let him first cast a stone at her.
And again he stooped down, and wrote on the ground.
And they which heard it, being convicted by their own conscience, went out one by one, beginning at the eldest, even unto the last: and Jesus was left alone, and the woman standing in the midst.
When Jesus had lifted up himself, and saw none but the woman, he said unto her, Woman, where are those thine accusers? Hath no man condemned thee?
She said, No man, Lord. And Jesus said unto her, Neither do I condemn thee: go, and sin no more.
Then spake Jesus again unto them, saying, I am the light of the world: he that followeth me shall not walk in darkness, but shall have the light of life".

Here, we learn of a woman who has sinned, and seeks forgiveness. Many would like to see her pay for her sin by being stoned to death. Jesus explains to the crowd that anyone who feels they are sinless may cast the first stone. With that one line, we are shown that no-one on this earth has the right to judge. It is an important and critical message of His gospel.

John 13:16

"Verily, verily, I say unto you, The servant is not greater than his lord; neither he that is sent greater than he that sent him".

Jesus here explains that all are equal, no-one is better than anyone else regardless of professional position or accomplishments. He also testifies he is no greater than his Father, which sent him to Earth.

John 13: 34&35
"A new commandment I give unto you, That ye love one another; as I have loved you, that ye also love one another. By this shall all men know that ye are my disciples, if ye have love one to another".
Further stating his gospel, Jesus commands that we are to love each other as he has love for you. That is our only obligation to each other, to be a friend.

John 16:7
"Nevertheless I tell you the truth; It is expedient for you that I go away: for if I go not away, the Comforter will not come unto you; but if I depart, I will send him unto you".
Jesus here is foretelling of the Crucifixion, that He will be leaving his disciples for a time, but that they will not be alone. It is important to understand that although we cannot see Him, He is indeed always with us.

John 19:28-30
"After this, Jesus knowing that all things were now accomplished, that the scripture might be fulfilled, saith, I thirst.
Now there was set a vessel full of vinegar: and they filled a sponge with vinegar, and put it upon hyssop, and put it to his mouth.
When Jesus therefore had received the vinegar, he said, It is finished: and he bowed his head, and gave up the ghost".
Perhaps regarded as an insignificant event in the last moments of His life, Jesus realises all things are accomplished and prepares to die. Fulfilling a Prophecy declared in the book of Psalms, Jesus tastes the vinegar (a drink given as customary to anyone being crucified, to slightly numb the

pain) and allows him to have enough moisture in his lips to say his final words, declaring the end of his mortal ministry.

As you can see from these very few select verses of a wide range of scripture, there was much written about Him by his followers, to allow people over 2000 years later to understand His legacy and His life. As the Ultimate Warrior so emotionally spoke about, the storytellers, or in Church context, the members, make that legacy continue by testifying of Him, and writing of Him.

This chapter can only end the way it begun, and by describing the life of Christ, a speech in the style of The Ultimate Warrior;

"Jesus Christ did not become glorified on his own. His Crucifixion and Atonement ended His life and His earthly mortal ministry. But it is what He did that makes us humble, thankful, believe and because of Him, we are saved. Our actions today make the life he led all for something. It is through our storytelling and example and loyalty that He is testified of today. Everyone reading this, everyone in any Church setting the world over, they are or can be a Disciple of Jesus Christ, by studying and living his teachings, and by being the example that He has set. The many Church members all over the world have the spirit with them, and they will continue to testify of him throughout all generations. He is Jesus Christ, He lives today as the Savior, you are examples of Jesus Christ, and the Ministry of Jesus Christ will run, forever!"

∞

This chapter is dedicated to all of the wrestlers who died so suddenly and shockingly, they will be immortalized and live forever through the storytellers. To name but a few – Eddie Guerrero (2005), 'Macho Man' Randy Savage (2011), 'Rowdy' Roddy Piper (2015), Dusty Rhodes (2015), The British Bulldog (2002), Owen Hart (1999) and of course, 'Ultimate Warrior' Jim Hellwig (2014). Earth's loss is Heaven's gain.

Chapter Ten

"Be Sure To Catch Me!"

The Parable of Co-Operation

Mosiah 18:21

"And he commanded them that there should be no contention one with another, but that they should look forward with one eye, having one faith and one baptism, having their hearts knit together in unity and in love one towards another"

Co-operation. It is a word used a lot in wrestling. We know wrestling is staged and the wrestlers are not actually out to hurt each other, they work together to perform the moves and make it look as realistic as possible to the fans. To do this, they have to co-operate and be in unity with each other, allowing their instructions to flow and perform the best match possible.

As discussed in the first chapter – "This is going to be Art!", the less experienced performers set up the move set beforehand and go through them as a rehearsed play, while the more experienced prefer go as the crowd and feeling directs. Sometimes, it doesn't go according to plan and sometimes something goes wrong. And sometimes, one person stops co-operating for reasons perhaps only known to the wrestler themselves.

For example, a young Lex Luger once fought the legendary Bruiser Brody in a cage match, way back in 1987. Some six minutes into the match, Brody stopped the pretence that he was being hurt by Lugers moves (known as 'selling') and did not flinch or move anytime Luger tried a punch or kick. Brody, who was reputed as a mad man in the ring, Luger rightfully feared for his safety. After trying a few more times to keep the match going, he spoke to the referee, shoved him down (calling for a disqualification loss) and ran out of the ring. Brody's actions of not co-operating and refusing to sell for his opponent ruined the match and the show for the paying fans. The legend is Brody did not like Luger, feeling he was too proud of himself and over entitled to any rewards, he refused to work with him and make him look good. Brusier Brody died a few years later after being stabbed in the backstage area of a wrestling show.

Scott Steiner had a reputation of 'taking liberties' with younger low card wrestlers in the final days of WCW. Having lost his sense of pride and professionalism in the crumbling mess that WCW had become, he took his anger and frustration out on others by punching them for real, roughing them up and slamming them with more force than normal. He got away with it too, due to the poor management at the time, and left some lasting effects on those he worked with.

And most famously, the feud between Shawn Michaels and Bret Hart turned real several times over the years, ending at Survivor Series in 1997 when the match ending was changed without Bret knowing...as you read in a previous chapter.

As you can see and imagine, when wrestlers stop co-operating and start fighting for real, due to tempers or real life hatred for each other, it can ruin a great match and even the entire show, as the audience expects a great match by two professionals. It's an unwritten rule in wrestling, as explained by Shawn Michaels at a recent show I attended, that if you get a reputation for not co-operating in matches, a wrestler would find himself blackballed from the business, what promoter would want to hire him if there was a chance he may legitimately hurt another wrestler or ruin the show for the paying fans.

It took me a long time to understand how the moves are completed without injuring the opponent. Yes there is always going to be some hurting and aching and broken bones, as the old saying goes – "This Ain't Ballet". I am not a trained wrestler and never will be, but over the past fifteen years through various TV shows highlighting the training one needs to be a wrestler, and watching shows from the front row, myself and many other fans have come to understand more of how a move is performed safely. It is all about co-operation, regarding your opponent's safety, timing and putting on a good show.

Most sequences require the wrestler taking the move to do most of the work. Take for example, the chokeslam. Watch carefully, you'll see it is the recipient, with the opponents hand around their neck, that is jumping up then landing back on the mat to devastating impact, while the wrestler giving the chokeslam follows their movement up and back down in time with them. A controlled landing and being able to fall without getting hurt is crucial to many of the higher impact moves such as a powerbomb, suplex and bodyslam. Working together to perform the move will provide a great show for all.

When all opponents concerned are united with the thought of performing the best match they can for the fans, keeping themselves and their opponent's safe, and timing everything correctly, it is guaranteed you will see a great match and a fantastic show. Watch almost any match with Bret Hart match for an example of this – he had a reputation of being one of the safest and smoothest workers in the business.

Sadly, a kick to the head from another wrestler, whose timing and execution were slightly off, ended his career. Clearly, co-operation is everything in terms of timing and execution.

∞

There are two parables that can be taken from this in regards to a Religious setting.
The first, is baptism. A baptism is symbolic of accepting Jesus Christ, cleansing of yourself from your old life and starting a new life under His guidance. By immersing yourself in the water fully and coming back up, you are presented 'clean' and sinless.
However, the road to an actual baptism can take months of scripture study, sincere prayer and conversation with other Church members before feeling ready. It is not something to be taken lightly, the person has to want to do it.
When being baptised, just as in wrestling, it is the person being baptised doing most of the work. Whoever is baptising them is simply a 'facilitator' if you will, to bring you back up from the water. The person being baptised must allow themselves to be laid under the water, if they are not willing then the person facilitating will have a very hard time getting them to go under! Once under, it is then through the co-operation of the facilitator to bring them back up, perhaps embrace in a hug, and the 'move' is completed. It all happens in mere seconds.
Secondly, there is no room for argument or division in any part of the Church. How can a Church unit with dissention and bad feelings appeal to any of its members as a place they want to be at, or even a new person joining. We are all human, and have those traits of anger and ego. However we are taught to control these and put the Savior first in any

Church setting, thus we will be unified with Him and co-operate with one another to run the Church correctly and the way He has instructed us. It really is that simple.

And just like with Lex Luger and Bruiser Brody, if one person decides not to co-operate or worse, cause trouble, it simply ruins the experience for everyone else there. Some may run away scared, as Luger did, never to return to Church again. And that is never the way Christ intended it.

Stone Cold Steve Austin said it best many years ago, "United We Stand, Divided We Fall!"

∞

This chapter is dedicated to the leaders I have served with over the years in my various Church callings, who taught me more than they realise. I also would like to mention Roy Hann, of Dundee, Scotland, who baptised me September 13th 2006.

Chapter Eleven

"If You're Afraid, You Won't Succeed!"

The Parable of Success And Failure

Alma 29:16

"Now, when I think of the success of these my brethren my soul is carried away, even to the separation of it from the body, as it were, so great is my joy"

We start this chapter with another great quote from Paul Heyman. This is taken from the DVD 'The Rise and Fall of ECW', the wrestling company that he owned and operated with great success until closure in 2001. Here, he is referencing the times he has failed only to come back with a something successful, time and time again.

"You cannot achieve success without the risk of failure. And I learned a long time ago, you cannot achieve success, if you fear failure. If you're not afraid to fail, man, you have a chance to succeed. But you're never gonna get there unless you risk it, all the way. I'll risk failure. Sometimes, half the fun is failing. Learning from your mistakes, waking up the next morning, and saying 'Okay. Watch out. Here I come again. A little bit smarter, licking my wounds, and really not looking forward to getting my butt kicked the way I just did yesterday.' So now, I'm just a little more dangerous"

An inspiring quote by a man who for six years gave his life to the company that was ECW. It was not an easy one to run, but he carried on until the very end. Countless problems on television and PPV deals, along with the usual scenarios any wrestling promoter has to deal with made running the shows sometimes a gruelling process. But, ask anyone who worked in ECW during Paul's years in charge to describe it all in one word, most would say – 'Fun'.

It's untimely demise in 2001, after the collapse due to lack of a television deal was a sad piece of news to hear. Paul was burned out from years of working twenty three hours a day, and the financial problems of the company were so severe they were forced to declare bankruptcy. It was a devastating end to a pioneering and captivating company, and for Paul who saw his dreams crumble. No-one would say he failed here; it was just that he could not compete with the larger wrestling companies. Many others tried to capture the heart of ECW in their own, smaller companies, but never managed to create the success that ECW had and will only ever have.

Paul, not one to give up, transitioned over to the WWF just one week after ECW closed its doors. Like the quote says, he picked himself up, and started again. This time, a little more educated than before. Going on to manage countless world Champions and most notably, Brock Lesnar, the man achieved more success than maybe even he thought possible.

∞

It's an inspiring and provoking quote, one that is mentioned by made hardcore wrestling fans years later, when explaining why Paul is 'The Godfather of Wrestling'. It is one I've put into practice and taught many times throughout Church classes. Perhaps it is more a motivational than a Religious based quote, but it still fits. It is human nature that sometimes we succeed, and sometimes we fail. It happens to the best of us. Every day we wake up and have plans and things we want to accomplish, and a lot of it might not work out the way we planned. We are risking failure to achieve that success. And yeah, sometimes half the fun is failing. We can only learn from our mistakes, they help us grow and make us stronger for next time. The beauty of any Religion is we can be forgiven for any mistakes we make as a person, it is all part of a learning process and part of a bigger plan.

In the Book of Genesis, we read about the fall of Adam and Eve. They were commanded not to eat from the tree of knowledge; however did so anyway after being tempted by Satan. God then cast them out of the Garden to fend for themselves, in doing so becoming mortal, able to experience good and evil. It was all part of a much bigger and greater plan, for it was to teach them and have them learn for themselves. They risked it all in the garden by partaking of the fruit, they did not fear failure (because they were not aware of it) and achieved the successful plan God had in store for them. They grew from this pivotal moment in the history of time and because of the fall, the world was able to progress to how it is today. 2 Nephi 2:27 states;

"Adam fell that men might be; and men are, that they might have joy"

Many people have short comings and areas of weakness, both Church members and non-believers. It is through those moments of failure we can achieve success, by understanding what we are doing wrong and coming back again, ready to tackle it with greater knowledge and power than last time! As we do so, we will have greater joy.

∞

This chapter is dedicated to Paul Heyman, a man that can turn sand into gold and live life to the full, he has carved out an amazing career.

Chapter Twelve

"Having Been Commissioned…"

The Parable of Continuance

Matthew 22: 37-38

"Jesus said unto him, Thou shalt love the Lord thy God with all thy heart, and with all thy soul, and with all thy mind. This is the first and great commandment"

So here we begin with another tale involving Shawn Michaels.

Going back to 1997, Shawn Michaels was the leader of the faction known as D-Generation X, with Triple H and Chyna. Known for their outlandish behaviour, rude skits and over the top promos, the talented Shawn was riding high as the WWF champion. Triple H was 'learning the ropes' from Shawn, preparing himself for main event status, while Chyna acted as an enforcer and bodyguard for the group.

After banishing his arch rival, Bret Hart, from the WWF, Shawn embarked on a prosperous reign as WWF Champion and the top wrestler in the company. His DX counterparts behind him, he was having a whale of a time on top. But it all came crashing down, literally, at the Royal Rumble a few short months later. While taking a fall out of the ring during a casket match (the object of the match being to lock your opponent in a casket for the win) against the Undertaker, Shawn landed wrongly and hit his back against the top of the casket. In incredible pain afterwards, he was put on light duties.

At Wrestlemania in March of 1998, Shawn lost the Championship to Stone Cold Steve Austin in an emotional and hard fought match. Despite being in tremendous pain, Shawn put on a show like only he can and gave the fans a match to remember. He quietly retired from the ring following this match, to heal his back and have surgery. It would be a very different company he would return too as an active wrestler some four years later.

But what did that mean for D-Generation X? Did Triple H and Chyna go their separate ways and move on from the group that Shawn worked so hard to establish and lead? Did Triple H forget everything he had learned from Shawn in terms of leadership skills and group unity? Did Chyna go and find something else to do with her time and forget where she came from?

Of course they didn't. Realising there is strength in numbers and it was now up to him to continue the DX name, Triple H appeared on Raw the night after Wrestlemania announcing that although Shawn may be gone, D Generation X will live on. Retaining the services of Chyna as the enforcer, Triple H recruited the returning Sean 'X-Pac' Waltman to the group, and later the team of the New Age Outlaws – Billy Gunn and Road Dogg. As a defined and unified group, they were able to wage war on similar groups within the company and command much television time each week. While under Shawn's leadership, they were defined as heels – the bad guys, mostly stemming from their part in Bret Hart's departure the previous year. But under the new leadership and direction, they were accepted by the fan base as faces – good guys who they could side with. The D-Generation X t-shirt sold in thousands, and no DX moment is more famous than the time they declared war on WCW, driving an army tank to a WCW Nitro one night that WWF was performing nearby, attempting to hijack the show and bring Triple H's buddies – Scott Hall and Kevin Nash back to the WWF. A hilarious and over the top scenario that had never been attempted before, it made for some great television and proved Triple H could lead the group into the future and establish himself (and the group) as a dominant force. Over the next few years, the group went through various incarnations as both faces and heels, different members joined and even Triple H left the group for a short time to further his career as a member of an opposing faction. However, upon Triple H winning the WWF championship in the summer of 1999, the group banded together once again as heels, to protect Triple H and his title reign. By the summer of 2000, all had gone their separate ways and the group was now defunct.

It would reform with Triple H and Shawn Michaels in 2006, with other original members joining in at various points. Never likely to be a full time group again, they still make sporadic appearances on television to further current storylines, most notably at Wrestlemania 31 to help Triple H battle and defeat Sting, it was a joyful and spectacular moment for the fans due to the history and legacy they have built.

  Shawn worked hard to establish the group in 1997. At the time of writing this book, it has been almost seventeen years the DX logo first graced our screens. And still, the legacy lives on. All members have carved out successful careers outside of the group, but credit their time inside it as a learning point and some of the best moments of their career. The fans still remember it with fondness, and appreciate the many great moments it has given us. It is the perfect example of how a wrestling group must carry themselves to remain relevant and unified. If it were not for Triple H taking the helm upon Shawn's retirement, there may not have been the DX we know and love today, it may have just been a distant memory, and the wrestling world would have been a very different place.

∞

  The actions and that which happened to the DX group can be likened to the situation that the original twelve Apostles found themselves in immediately following the Saviors death on the cross.

  As you read in a previous chapter, Jesus performed many great actions and taught various principles throughout the establishment and running of His church. He had his disciples and followers and was able to carve out a glorious few years as the perfect leader and teacher.

It is thanks to an inspiring and thought out talk by LDS Apostle; Elder Jeffery R. Holland, and relentless studying of John 21 that this chapter has come about.

Much like the original incarnation of D-Generation X, the Church that Jesus Christ established and the Apostles and members which followed him, found itself and themselves without a leader, upon the Savior's Crucifixion and burial. After teaching them and performing the Atonement – the saving ordinance for all mankind, they unwittingly assumed that the work was completed. It even states in John chapter 20, that Jesus Christ himself uttered the words – "It is finished!"

While Triple H, as the remaining senior member of DX, took it upon himself to continue the work that Shawn had started, the senior Apostle Peter had other plans upon the death his Master, so it seemed.

John 21:3

"Simon Peter saith unto them, I go a fishing. They say unto him, We also go with thee. They went forth, and entered into a ship immediately; and that night they caught nothing."

The remaining Apostles looked to Peter for advice on what to do next. Looking at this verse, and based on Elder Hollands informative and powerful interpretation of the chapter, Peter decided to return to his previous life of a fisherman. Some of the other Apostles would follow him, intending to return to their old lives as fisherman as well. But, on that night, they did not catch one single fish.

John 21: 4-6
"But when the morning was now come, Jesus stood on the shore: but the disciples knew not that it was Jesus.
Then Jesus saith unto them, Children, have ye any meat? They answered him, No.
And he said unto them, Cast the net on the right side of the ship, and ye shall find. They cast therefore, and now they were not able to draw it for the multitude of fishes."

The Apostles turned again fisherman are asked by a stranger on the shore how much fish they were able to catch. However, they were unaware, perhaps due to distance or the dark sky, that the stranger was in fact the resurrected Jesus Christ. The stranger instructs them to cast the net again, on the right side, to find their catch. In doing so, they are filled.

Here, we remember the first meeting of Peter and Jesus Christ, documented in Luke chapter 5, where Peter had been unable to catch any fish all night long. Jesus stepped into the boat with Peter and his crew of other fisherman, and taught them His Gospel. Following this, Jesus instructed Peter to cast his net out once again. Although explaining that they had worked all night and caught nothing, he did as asked. Almost immediately, his net was filled. Peter and his fellow crew gave up the life of fisherman to become 'fishers of men', that is, Apostles of Jesus Christ.

John 21:7-8
"Therefore that disciple whom Jesus loved saith unto Peter, It is the Lord. Now when Simon Peter heard that it was the Lord, he girt his fisher's coat unto him, (for he was naked,) and did cast himself into the sea.
And the other disciples came in a little ship; (for they were not far from land, but as it were two hundred cubits,) dragging the net with fishes."

Peter, remembering the miracle of before, realised who the stranger was and went to meet him. The remaining fisherman followed, dragging the nets of fish with them. Christ has returned in his immortal and resurrected state, to converse with his Apostles.

John 21:12-13
"Jesus saith unto them, Come and dine. And none of the disciples durst ask him, Who art thou? knowing that it was the Lord.
Jesus then cometh, and taketh bread, and giveth them, and fish likewise."

Though it may have seemed almost impossible, the fisherman turned again Apostles found themselves back with the Savior, and continuing the example he had taught previously, He served them with food. There was no question by any of the Apostles about who he was.

Now in DX, when Shawn left and was no longer the leader, the group continued in different forms over the years, with

Shawn eventually returning as a leader once again. Here, the Apostles continued to work together as fisherman, until Jesus Christ returned and taught them the principle of continuing the Ministry and Gospel of Jesus Christ, even when their glorious leader could not be with them anymore. In these next three verses, Jesus asks this question to Peter, allowing him to realise for himself that this great work shall indeed go on.

John 21: 15-17

"So when they had dined, Jesus saith to Simon Peter, Simon, son of Jonas, lovest thou me more than these? He saith unto him, Yea, Lord; thou knowest that I love thee. He saith unto him, Feed my lambs.
He saith to him again the second time, Simon, son of Jonas, lovest thou me? He saith unto him, Yea, Lord; thou knowest that I love thee. He saith unto him, Feed my sheep.
He saith unto him the third time, Simon, son of Jonas, lovest thou me? Peter was grieved because he said unto him the third time, Lovest thou me? And he said unto him, Lord, thou knowest all things; thou knowest that I love thee. Jesus saith unto him, Feed my sheep."

Jesus is enquiring of Peter, asking him to search his heart and acknowledge his love and devotion for him, and if he is willing to continue the work they started, more than going back to being a fisherman.

Elder Holland explained this further, in his non-scriptural but eye opening elaboration which picks up following Jesus saying for the second time – "Feed my sheep" as follows;

""Then Peter, why are you here? Why are we back on this same shore, by these same nets, having this same conversation? Wasn't it obvious then and isn't it obvious now that if I want fish, I can get fish? What I need, Peter, are disciples—and I need them forever. I need someone to feed my sheep and save my lambs. I need someone to preach my gospel and defend my faith. I need someone who loves me, truly, truly loves me, and loves what our Father in Heaven has commissioned me to do. Ours is not a feeble message. It is not a fleeting task. It is not hapless; it is not hopeless; it is not to be consigned to the ash heap of history. It is the work of Almighty God, and it is to change the world. So, Peter, for the second and presumably the last time, I am asking you to leave all this and to go teach and testify, labor and serve loyally until the day in which they will do to you exactly what they did to me.

Then, turning to all the Apostles, He might well have said something like: "Were you as foolhardy as the scribes and Pharisees? As Herod and Pilate? Did you, like they, think that this work could be killed simply by killing me? Did you, like they, think the cross and the nails and the tomb were the end of it all and each could blissfully go back to being whatever you were before? Children, did not my life and my love touch your hearts more deeply than this?"

D-Generation X was not ready to disband and fade away once their great leader had departed, no more than the Apostles were ready to disband and go their separate ways following the death of the Savior. Despite only a few years of learning and following their Master, they were ready and established to carry on this great work. Jesus Christ returned to remind them of this and demonstrate their love and commitment to Him.

If it were not for the events described in this chapter, the Ministry of Jesus Christ may have ended forever at this point, and the world would have been a much more different and challenging place.

∞

This chapter is dedicated to my close circle of friends – Steven, Joe, Colin, Steve and Daniel. Through our association and friendship, we have made many great memories together.

Chapter Thirteen

"Like A Dormant Volcano"

The Parable Of Preparation

Alma 34:32-33

"For behold, this life is the time for men to prepare to meet God; yea, behold the day of this life is the day for men to perform their labours.
And now, as I said unto you before, as ye have had so many witnesses, therefore, I beseech of you that ye do not procrastinate the day of your repentance until the end; for after this day of life, which is given us to prepare for eternity, behold, if we do not improve our time while in this life, then cometh the night of darkness wherein there can be no labour performed."

Another ingenious speech from Paul Heyman opens up this chapter, concerning his handicap match that coming week where he teams with Ryback to take on CM Punk, in September 2013. Paul certainly has a way with words and finding the right ones to make the audience listen. Reading it here does not do it justice by the way, take a look for it on the internet to fully appreciate it. Here, he compares himself to a volcano, ready to unleash danger on those that dare to cross him...

"Sunday, Sunday, Sunday! It's an execution live on WWE pay-per-view, as "The Best in the World" CM Punk straps me into the electric chair, puts the poison into my veins, lines me up in front of the firing squad and pulls the trigger himself! For the first time ever — and for the first time ever again — it will never, ever happen ... as a non-participant gets locked inside of a cell with a man who doesn't spend his night fantasizing about the Diiiiivas. CM Punk spends his night fantasizing and obsessing about the massacre he wants to inflict upon Paul Heyman. CM Punk wants to take me down, take me out, DRIVE ME AWAY from WWE forever.

But just like when a volcano is trapped inside of a dormant mountain. When that volcano finally erupts and the lava — the molten lava — drips down the side of the mountain ... I'm just like that lava! I'm red-hot! I'm out of control! And all of the villagers, with the lava pouring down into their houses, destroying their cars, suffocating and melting their flesh, and the villagers are going "run for your lives, run for your lives, run for your lives!" They're the ones that love and worship CM Punk! And I'm the one ... that has a different strategy.

Because I'm not all filled with emotion like CM Punk, Renee. I'm cold-hearted. And I'm calculated. And I'm in control ... the same way I've controlled CM Punk all of these years. The same way I control my monster, Ryback. And CM Punk cannot get past my monster, Ryback, which means CM Punk can't get his hands on me. Which is why Sunday, Sunday, Sunday, I'm not locked in a cell with CM Punk, CM Punk is locked in a cell with me."

What exactly is Paul saying here? It may look to be all over the place, wild, crazy, outrageous and slightly insane, but then, that was Paul Heyman at his best.

The start entails exactly what the fans are thinking, that come Sunday, CM Punk will destroy Paul Heyman and banish him from WWE forever. Only from his mind can he describe it so brilliantly, and explain how badly CM Punk wants to be rid of him. He goes on to talk about a volcano, how it can erupt without warning, and destroy everything quickly. The villagers are unprepared for the eruption, and suffered because of it. He finally explains he is in control, and prepared for anything that can come his way. He has protection and he has a plan. And anything (or anyone) facing him should be the one who is scared.

It was the middle part that really stood out to me, the dormant mountain followed by the eruption of lava, and nothing can be done to stop it from pouring out. One moment, the villagers are fine and next, literally, 'running for their lives'. Paul loves to talk about having a strategy, having knowledge, having sources to help him overcome that which is opposing him. He was prepared for anything and everything that would come his way, he's just that good.

Alas, this being wrestling, the bad guys loose most of the time. Paul (the heel) and Ryback (also heel) were beaten by

CM Punk the following week, in a savage and brutal way. Perhaps Paul was too confident, or maybe Punk was too much to overcome. Either way, Paul did the job he always does and will continue to do, he made it worth watching.

∞

  Preparation and knowledge are key fundamentals that any Church teaches. People the world over, in practically any Church, attend to seek guidance and learn more of spiritual matters. Paul spoke in his promo of being prepared and ready to face anything that came at him, no matter how big or small he would use a brilliant strategy to deal with it, he always had a plan.
  On that, I will speak here regarding the second coming of the Savior - Jesus Christ. Just as importantly, I will address how we are taught to prepare accordingly, based upon what Paul (Heyman) has said above.
  Much like the volcano trapped inside the dormant mountain, that no-one can say for certain when it will erupt, the same can be said about the second coming. We are counselled and taught that the second coming is near, but that nobody, not even his Prophet or the Pope or any well-known Religious leader can say for certain when it shall be. Unlike the eruption of the deathly lava, it is an event that any Christian will look forward too with gladness and joy. As stated in Isaiah 25:9, regarding the Saviors first presence on earth;

"And it shall be said in that day, Lo, this is our God; we have waited for him, and he will save us: this is the Lord; we have waited for him, we will be glad and rejoice in his salvation."

And in Matthew 1:21;

"Behold, the angel of the Lord appeared unto him in a dream, saying, Joseph, thou son of David, fear not to take unto thee Mary thy wife: for that which is conceived in her is of the Holy Ghost.
And she shall bring forth a son, and thou shalt call his name Jesus: for he shall save his people from their sins.
Now all this was done, that it might be fulfilled which was spoken of the Lord by the prophet, saying,
Behold, a virgin shall be with child, and shall bring forth a son, and they shall call his name Emmanuel, which being interpreted is, God with us."

    The scriptures teach that Jesus Christ is not here to destroy us or the world, or to cause pain and suffering, but here to save us from the world itself, from the pain and suffering. He will spare us from our sins as we seek forgiveness, and shall be with us forever.

    As discussed in a previous chapter of this book, and throughout the entire New Testament and other approved scripture, Jesus Christ came to the earth as prophesised, established his Ministry and performed the Atonement, thereby completing what he was sent here to do by God himself. And it is prophesised that he will return again, in his perfect and glorious state of capacity, to rule over the earth in Peace.

Like Paul Heyman would develop strategy and guidance to help him in any situation (even though he didn't always win, that's wrestling) so can we, the people of earth, be ready for the second coming by following that which is printed in scripture and given to us by Church leaders.   There are many signs that the second coming is drawing nearer and nearer, even the official name of the church being 'The Church Of Jesus Christ Of Latter-Day Saints' (it being Christ's Church, and these believed to the last days before his grand return).

The scriptures prophecy of evil, wickedness and destruction on the earth during the last day;

"And ye shall hear of wars and rumours of wars: see that ye be not troubled: for all these things must come to pass, but the end is not yet."
Matthew 24:6

"And ye shall hear of wars and rumours of wars: see that ye be not troubled: for all these things must come to pass, but the end is not yet."
Matthew 24:7

"And then shall many be offended, and shall betray one another, and shall hate one another."
Matthew 24:10

"And this gospel of the kingdom shall be preached in all the world for a witness unto all nations; and then shall the end come."
Matthew 24:14

"For there shall arise false Christs, and false prophets, and shall show great signs and wonders; insomuch that, if it were possible, they shall deceive the very elect."
Matthew 24:24

Those above are a few short verses from the book of Matthew, in the New Testament. Jesus explains to his disciples the signs of his second coming – wars, evil speaking and hating of one another, betrayal, false Prophets and confusion over Religion, and somewhere Christ's correct Gospel will be preached, eventually reaching the entire world.

Jesus explains later in the chapter, in the most beautiful and uplifting way, exactly how he will appear at the second coming (verses 29-31);

"Immediately after the tribulation of those days shall the sun be darkened, and the moon shall not give her light, and the stars shall fall from heaven, and the powers of the heavens shall be shaken.
And then shall appear the sign of the Son of man in heaven: and then shall all the tribes of the earth mourn, and they shall see the Son of man coming in the clouds of heaven with power and great glory.
And he shall send his angels with a great sound of a trumpet, and they shall gather together his elect from the four winds, from one end of heaven to the other."

As we experience the trials and tribulations, the sadness and confusion explained in the above verses of Matthew, whilst looking forward to Christ's second coming, we must prepare in every way possible for this day. Elder Dallin H. Oaks quoted in his talk from General Conference April 2004

(Preparation For The Second Coming) on the parable of preparedness regarding the ten virgins (given in Matthew 25);

"A parable that contains an important and challenging teaching on this subject is the parable of the ten virgins. Of this parable, the Lord said, "And at that day, when I shall come in my glory, shall the parable be fulfilled which I spake concerning the ten virgin.
Given in the 25th chapter of Matthew, this parable contrasts the circumstances of the five foolish and the five wise virgins. All ten were invited to the wedding feast, but only half of them were prepared with oil in their lamps when the bridegroom came. The five who were prepared went into the marriage feast, and the door was shut. The five who had delayed their preparations came late. The door had been closed, and the Lord denied them entrance, saying, "I know you not". "Watch therefore," the Savior concluded, "for ye know neither the day nor the hour wherein the Son of man cometh" .
The arithmetic of this parable is chilling. The ten virgins obviously represent members of Christ's Church, for all were invited to the wedding feast and all knew what was required to be admitted when the bridegroom came. But only half were ready when he came."

There is no doubt, based on the New Testament alone, that we must be ready for the return of the Savior, and on that great and glorious day be ready to meet him.

This life on earth has been called a time to prepare to meet Jesus Christ and enter into God's presence once again. Only by seeking and studying his words, and striving to live the principles he has taught can we be ready to meet him. As we learn of him and come to appreciate him more, we will learn of his love for us and come to love him more. By doing so, our love for others will grow too. The righteous shall gather as the gospel is taken to more people, and the wickedness and evil of the world can and will be destroyed, little by little.

Of course, everyone has faults and weaknesses. Everybody makes mistakes, everybody succumbs to evilness at some stage. But through Jesus Christ, this can be overcome by recognizing and repenting of our mistakes (and this will be discussed in greater detail in the final chapter).

My final thought here comes from a Church meeting which I was not present at but told about later. Our then Stake President, Daryl Watson, asked those in attendance a question – "When do you think the second coming will be?" A few answers were raised, such as in ten years, twenty years, another hundred years etc. Daryl then explained with great passion (I'm told) that "As far as you are concerned, the second coming is tomorrow!" As explained above, nobody can be certain when it will be, just that the signs show it will be soon. By keeping ourselves prepared and worthy, and by continually studying the scriptures and keeping those commandments that have been set for us, can we be ready. We are all mortal and can death can find us any point, and it seems here that Daryl counselled us to live each day as our last. The Savior may return tomorrow, our mortal lives may

end tomorrow, but we should be able to look back and say we did everything we were instructed to, to be ready to meet The Savior.
Doctrine and Covenants 33:17-18 states

"Wherefore," the Savior tells us, "be faithful, praying always, having your lamps trimmed and burning, and oil with you, that you may be ready at the coming of the Bridegroom—For behold, verily, verily, I say unto you, that I come quickly"

∞

This chapter is dedicated to every Prophet and Apostle that serves or has served the people of earth. It is from their revelations and continued revelation today by which we are able to become so prepared.

Chapter Fourteen

"Your Tag Team Partner – God!"

The Parable Of The Teams

LDS Hymn Book Number 260 – "Who's on the Lord's Side"

"Who's on the Lord's side? Who?
Now is the time to show.
We ask it fearlessly:
Who's on the Lord's side? Who"

    In all my years as a fan of pro-wrestling, I have been some controversial storylines and angles broadcast on the television shows. There has been kidnapping of wives/valets, crazed lunatics wielding a gun at their opponent, fighting over custody of children, and exploiting alcohol and substance abuse. The general rule in wrestling is, if they can make money from it and draw a crowd, they'll run with it.
  As explained in a previous chapter "The Omega Lineup", Religion has been exploited by promoters as well. All characters in this sense have come across as smarmy (Brother Love), evil (The Undertakers satanic days) or corrupt (The Reverend D-Von). This author admits however they were never anything less than entertaining. They are simply people playing a character on a television show, they are not created to offend, though some critics say the opposite.

Perhaps only Shawn Michaels has been allowed to portray his Religious beliefs in a positive light while on television. Frequently, he would slip in references to his faith (his wrestling tights usually had crosses on them, he would hold his hands in the air and pray to God before a match, t-shirts had Religious symbols etc.) and it was generally well respected.

In early 2006, Shawn had been feuding with Vince McMahon and his son Shane (his bosses and the 'heels' in this situation) in the storyline. Following Shawn defeating Vince at Wrestlemania 22 in an outstanding and attention grabbing contest, new boundaries were reached. Vince claimed it had become a handicap match at Wrestlemania, with him having to face Shawn and the Almighty God himself. He claimed that God was helping Shawn the whole time, and had an unfair advantage in doing so!

So, Vince McMahon, being the over the top and slightly psychotic character he had become known as, declared on an episode of Raw a new Religion – "McMahonism". Oh yes, he was now worshipping himself and encouraging others to do likewise. Through his own personal Religion, he claimed he could destroy Shawn Michaels once and for all, and not even God could stop him. He then booked a tag team match at the next major show, Backlash, where Vince and Shane would team up to take on Shawn Michaels and his tag team partner – God.

Would 'God' show up at Backlash? It would be some sight if he did. On the day of the show, the McMahons entered first, looking very confident. Before Shawn could make his entrance, Vince introduced Shawn's tag team partner, 'God'. With that, holy music played over the loudspeakers and the spotlight made its way down the ramp and around the ring. This, we were meant to believe, was God himself making an entrance. Vince even ordered the music to be changed to something more 'jiggy' as he was in McMahon's arena now. Shawn then made his entrance, brimming with confidence as always. It was essentially a handicap match. Shawn vs The McMahons. 'God' did not even tag into the match, and the odds were worsened for Shawn when the Spirit Squad, a group of five male wrestling cheerleaders interfered to help the McMahons. After a long beating by Shawn on both McMahons, the match ended with the entire spirit squad hoisting Shawn into the air and sending him crashing through a table, for Vince to then pin him. It was followed by an evil look from Vince, and a fantastic line from commentator Jerry Lawler – "Victory for the Father, the Son and the Holy Spirit Squad".

The whole thing was so absurd and hilarious to watch unfold. It was always going to be a handicap match, with Vince (as the bad guy) mocking Shawn (the good guy) and his beliefs to try and get under his skin. It did not work of course, as evidenced by Shawn's entrance and fighting performance throughout the entire match. I can only defend and praise the entire angle here. It generated a lot of interest in the match itself, and that is really the purpose of any angle in wrestling – it makes the audience care about what they are watching, instead of just watching it.

In numerous interviews since then, including the day I met him, Shawn has defended the angle. He has said a lot of praise was heaped on WWE at the time for speaking about Religion on the show, and for it not to be portrayed in a distasteful way. He has said as well the whole thing was so over the top and comical, that it did not bother him in any way. He understands it was just part of a show and revelled in it.

As stated in previous chapters though, wrestling being wrestling, even with the help of God or any other Religious icons, the bad guys do sometimes win. But, that is what keeps us fans coming back for more each time.

∞

If we were able to choose a tag team partner for life, who would it be? Someone to help us battle through the daily trials and tribulations, the upset and anger, the hurt and malice, who would we choose?
There is a well-known poem I will share here, which is popular among many Christian groups and illustrates that the tag team partner is the Savior, Jesus Christ.

*"One night I dreamed a dream.
As I was walking along the beach with my Lord.
Across the dark sky flashed scenes from my life.
For each scene, I noticed two sets of footprints in the sand,
One belonging to me and one to my Lord.*

*After the last scene of my life flashed before me,
I looked back at the footprints in the sand.
I noticed that at many times along the path of my life,
especially at the very lowest and saddest times,
there was only one set of footprints.*

*This really troubled me, so I asked the Lord about it.
"Lord, you said once I decided to follow you,
You'd walk with me all the way.
But I noticed that during the saddest and most troublesome times of my life,*

there was only one set of footprints.
I don't understand why, when I needed You the most, You would leave me."

He whispered, "My precious child, I love you and will never leave you
Never, ever, during your trials and testings.
When you saw only one set of footprints,
It was then that I carried you."
(Credit – Mary Stevenson)

In the world of wrestling, sometimes the more experienced member of a tag team will carry the opponent during the match. They have been around longer, and maybe know and understand their opponents better. When their partner is out of his depth, he will be able to help him to win the match and claim victory. So too in life, as illustrated by the above poem, we are helped by the Lord in difficult and stressful times.

He can and will 'carry' us when we are at our lowest, our most troubled. When we face trials and tests of faith, it is then that we feel his presence most in our lives. I have felt it many times in my own life, and have friends who have felt it as well.

There is a famous picture which illustrates my point in this chapter (legal rights prevent me from publishing said picture). It shows Jesus and a boy sitting on a park bench together. They are not sitting facing each other nor are they are sitting away from each other. They are sitting together, side by side, discussing something with each other. There is a sense of calm and peace between them, where they can share anything. When we are struggling, feeling down or otherwise afflicted, picture yourself on this bench, sitting side by side with the Savior himself, ready to take on whatever problems you have – together.

He will never steer you wrong, he is the greatest tag team partner you will ever have, and to quote Philippians 4:13, with him – "All things are possible to those who believe".

∞

This chapter is dedicated to all those all who serve in a stewardship capacity in the Church, representing Jesus Christ to those whom they serve. Without naming them, there have been many that guided me in times of distress and hardship. I thank you from the bottom of my heart.

Chapter Fifteen

"Light vs Darkness"

The Parable Of Good vs Evil

Psalms 23:4

"Yea, though I walk through the valley of the shadow of death, I will fear no evil: for thou art with me; thy rod and thy staff they comfort me."

It is safe to say that Shawn Michaels really has been a huge influence in my life, as many chapters of this book use his work in wrestling to illustrate the lesson. He has done so much, seen every opponent and participated in every scenario in his historic career.

We open this chapter in March 2009, preparing for the grandest event of the year – Wrestlemania. Shawn at this time, is a very content and happy man, he describes himself as 'living Heaven on earth'. He feels he is ready to take on any challenge, and with Wrestlemania coming up, the only challenge he wants is The Undertaker. Well known for having 'The Streak', being undefeated at Wrestlemania 16-0 at this point, Shawn felt it was his time, that he could battle and defeat Undertaker on the biggest stage of them all. He laid out the challenge, claiming although Undertaker was undefeated at Wrestlemania, he was 'Mr Wrestlemania' – having had the best match on the show nearly each year.

The Undertaker, never being one to be afraid, accepted the match and exclaimed to Shawn – "Sometimes, it's hell trying to get to Heaven!" He also claimed the time for prayer had only just begun, thereby cementing the fact that Shawn will not have an easy night.

The foundations laid, the build-up over the next month to Wrestlemania was filled with Religious overtones and symbols. The Undertaker has long represented darkness and fear, even being called 'The Devil's favourite demon'. Here, it was no different. Meanwhile, Shawn took to wearing pure white most weeks on television and represented the light. The beginning of Genesis chapter one was quoted by Shawn to illustrate their differences;

" In the beginning God created the heaven and the earth. And the earth was without form, and void; and darkness was upon the face of the deep. And the Spirit of God moved upon the face of the waters.
And God said, Let there be light: and there was light. And God saw the light, that it was good: and God divided the light from the darkness."

Shawn claimed he feared no evil, and had victory over death, Hell and the grave. He claimed to have eternal life and was not afraid – signifying his confidence of defeating Undertaker.

The Undertaker responded by informing Shawn that the gates of Hell were open, that he was the most dangerous entity to ever set foot in wrestling. He explained, menacingly, that all who have tried to slay him at Wrestlemania have fallen at his feet, one by one. And Shawn would be no different; he would 'Rest In Peace'.

It was a fantastic build-up to what was sure to be a match of the year candidate, and different from others where a new slant was put on it to signify their characters more to the audience. The symbolism continued at Wrestlemania, when Shawn made his entrance from the top of the building – a spotlight on him as he descended 'from the heavens' on a platform, to some very heavenly music. Meanwhile, Undertaker appeared from underneath the building, to his terrifying entrance sound – signifying the evilness and destruction that he brings.

And with that, the build-up and grand entrances over, the match began. What followed was a five star wrestling contest by two of the greatest performers ever. Almost a half hour after the starting bell, The Undertaker was able to use his tombstone piledriver finishing manoeuvre to pin Shawn and win the match. Everything about this shows why we love wrestling – the logical story, the memorable entrances, the gripping battle of two cast iron and completely different warriors, and the classic match they put together. It has since been voted the greatest match in Wrestlemania history.

∞

The opening scripture to this chapter, taken from Psalms and quoted by Shawn during the build-up is the perfect passage to illustrate this parable. That, along with the roles played by Shawn and Undertaker illustrates a battle that is played out daily all over the world, namely good vs evil.

The reality of their roles is simple – the world is embroiled in the battle of Jesus Christ and Satan. We can choose to walk in the light of Christ and have eternal salvation, or we can choose to follow Satan himself and live in the darkness forever. By keeping the commandments set before us, we are promised protection from Satan and his forceful ways. Satan has the power to deceive and hurt us, taking a commandment and letting us justify breaking it. After the repercussions are felt, he sees that we are down and finds more ways to hurt us. Only through Jesus Christ can we be steered correctly.

A scripture that illustrates the powers of both figures and the blessings of staying in the light are found in the Book Of Mormon, in chapter seven of Moroni (verses 10-19);

"Wherefore, a man being evil cannot do that which is good; neither will he give a good gift.
For behold, a bitter fountain cannot bring forth good water; neither can a good fountain bring forth bitter water; wherefore, a man being a servant of the devil cannot follow Christ; and if he follow Christ he cannot be a servant of the devil.
Wherefore, all things which are good cometh of God; and that which is evil cometh of the devil; for the devil is an enemy unto God, and fighteth against him continually, and inviteth and enticeth to sin, and to do that which is evil continually.
But behold, that which is of God inviteth and enticeth to do good continually; wherefore, everything which inviteth and enticeth to do good, and to love God, and to serve him, is inspired of God.
Wherefore, take heed, my beloved brethren, that ye do not judge that which is evil to be of God, or that which is good and of God to be of the devil.
For behold, my brethren, it is given unto you to judge, that ye may know good from evil; and the way to judge is as plain, that ye may know with a perfect knowledge, as the daylight is from the dark night.
For behold, the Spirit of Christ is given to every man, that he may know good from evil; wherefore, I show unto you the

way to judge; for everything which inviteth to do good, and to persuade to believe in Christ, is sent forth by the power and gift of Christ; wherefore ye may know with a perfect knowledge it is of God.
But whatsoever thing persuadeth men to do evil, and believe not in Christ, and deny him, and serve not God, then ye may know with a perfect knowledge it is of the devil; for after this manner doth the devil work, for he persuadeth no man to do good, no, not one; neither do his angels; neither do they who subject themselves unto him.
And now, my brethren, seeing that ye know the light by which ye may judge, which light is the light of Christ, see that ye do not judge wrongfully; for with that same judgment which ye judge ye shall also be judged.
Wherefore, I beseech of you, brethren, that ye should search diligently in the light of Christ that ye may know good from evil; and if ye will lay hold upon every good thing, and condemn it not, ye certainly will be a child of Christ."

A bitter fountain cannot bring forth good water! We cannot deceive Christ, and we cannot deceive Satan. We cannot serve two masters. We must choose for ourselves, by using the knowledge and that which we learn further through study to decide whom to serve.

By following the light of Christ and finding joy in serving him and living his teachings, we shall find eternal salvation (as Shawn spoke of). We will all encounter Satan and his temptations at some stage (in this parable represented by The Undertaker), and through that which we know to be good and right and wholesome he can be overcome. Sometimes, we may taste defeat as Shawn did this time, and give into temptation. But the beauty of choosing Christ is that his light never ever goes out, it really is eternal. Through continued repentance and prayer, this can be and is always possible.

∞

This chapter is dedicated to all those behind the Shawn Michaels vs Undertaker matchup, who through their spectacular form of entertainment were able to take a centuries old battle and make it into a compelling story for Wrestlemania. For them, there is no greater compliment.

Chapter Sixteen

"If I Can't Beat You...I Have No Career!"

The Parable Of Focus

Matthew 25:23

"His Lord said unto him, Well done, good and faithful servant; thou hast been faithful over a few things, I will make thee ruler over many things: enter thou into the joy of thy lord."

My thoughts in this chapter concern God's instruction to focus on what matters most in life, and not obsessing over that which will do us harm in the grand scheme of things. We are commanded to live a joyful and productive life, obeying that which has been set forth for us and generally using our time wisely to further our needs and God's plan. Sometimes however, we can become some so obsessed with one thing in life, so consumed and focused on it that we maybe forget everything else and loose that which we love in the process.

To illustrate this, I bring two examples from wrestling. One is from a storyline, showing how much can be lost, while the other is a real life story of someone so consumed with his life as a wrestler, he admits to having forgotten about anything and everything else.

In the previous chapter, we saw how Shawn Michaels and The Undertaker built up their match for Wrestlemania through a light vs darkness parable in the storyline. Shawn, after a valiant effort, lost the match. Fast forward nine months later, Shawn decided he wanted to try again. After accepting an award for his match of the year with Undertaker, the wheels turned inside his head and he challenged him again, a rematch at the next Wrestlemania.

The Undertaker confronted him later, and declined his challenge. A reason was not given, we can only assume because he beat him the previous year that Undertaker wanted a new challenge. With that, Shawn declared he would enter the Royal Rumble match that year. If he won, it would allow him to headline Wrestlemania against the Champion, who at the time was – The Undertaker. Entering another speciality performance in the Royal Rumble, Shawn gave it his all! Like a man possessed, a man obsessed with winning so he could face (and beat) The Undertaker, he fought valiantly, even eliminating his best friend, Triple H. But, it would not be that easy, and he was eliminated by the wrestler Batista. After a few moments of looking sorrowful and on the verge of breakdown, he snapped and beat up referees before being escorted away from the ring. The next few weeks saw him break down ever further – further attacks on referees, ego getting the better of him by trying to show off in a tag team match, leading to he and Triple H losing their tag team titles. He faced fines, suspensions and would not focus on the matches at hand. All he could think about was beating The Undertaker, it consumed him and ate at his soul, being the one thing he was so desperate to accomplish. After arguing with Triple H and disbanding DX, then beating up more officials backstage, Shawn announced his career was over. If he could not face The Undertaker, he had no career he claimed, and walked out of WWE.

But, still itching away at his soul, Shawn returned a few weeks later with a sure fire plan to get his match. While The Undertaker defended his WWE Championship in the Elimination Chamber matchup, Shawn snuck in and superkicked him, allowing him to be pinned by his opponent and loose the championship. As the referee counted the three, Shawn looked down at what he had done. Not moving, his face showed a look of sadness and guilt. He knew in his mind that he had done wrong, but for the good of his career it had to be done. Now, without the title, Undertaker would have to find someone else to compete against at Wrestlemania. Shawn knew Undertaker would want revenge, and would accept his challenge for Wrestlemania. His plan had worked.

Or so he thought.

Undertaker did accept the challenge, the match was set. Undertaker vs Shawn Michaels, Wrestlemania edition part II. However, Undertaker accepted on one condition: Shawn had to put his career on the line. Streak vs career, legend vs legend. Shawn, willing to do anything to get the match and convinced in his obsessed mind that he could beat him, accepted. He further claimed that if he could not beat Undertaker, he had no career. This clearly meant everything to him.

And on the night, they wrested as perfect a match as the year before. Going on last, the crowd was hooked on their every move and exchange. An emotionally charged contest, fans were behind both men, cheering them on. It was the final few moments that really struck home. Shawn, battered and bruised, would not stay down when Undertaker had the better of him. As Undertaker was about to pick Shawn up and deliver an anticipated match winning tombstone piledriver, he looked down at Shawn, lying on the canvas. And he felt sorry for him, that this man was so obsessed with beating him and would not give up. He would not quit. He screamed at Shawn to stay down, to end it. Shawn, defiant to the very end, used Undertaker to pull himself up off the canvas. He then gestured to him that HIS end was near and slapped Undertaker, hard, across the face. With that, Undertaker's sympathy disappeared, and he delivered the tombstone piledriver to Shawn. Three seconds later, it was over. Shawn lost, his career was over. He put everything on the line for this one match that he was so obsessed to have, and lost. I remember watching it unfold live, with a room full of other wrestling fans, and I admit we all shed a tear to see him loose. He was a hero to us all.

Thankfully, it ends on a happy note. In a real life, unscripted moment on the show, Undertaker picked Shawn up off the canvas, shook his hand and they embraced in a hug. It was as real a moment as you'll ever see on a wrestling show. At that point I cried, as did many other fans around the world. The Undertaker left the ring, and allowed Shawn to bask in the glory one last time. Despite playing a tweener bad guy in the last few weeks of his career, it was all forgotten about as the crowd gave applause for Shawn and thanked him for his amazing career and the legacy he would leave behind. The emotion doesn't get more real than that night.

My second illustration concerns one of the greatest wrestlers of the 80's and 90's, the legendary Jake 'The Snake' Roberts. A highly intelligent performer, he knew exactly where to be and what to do at all times in the ring, he was well respected among fellow colleagues for it. However, as years passed, time on the road took its toll and the injuries mounted. He came to rely on drugs, alcohol and other adverse substances. His career entered a tailspin in the late 90's and all through the 2000's, until seeking help from fellow wrestler and self-help specialist – Diamond Dallas Page. After months of rehabilitation, help and support from his family and friends, he was inducted into the WWE Hall of Fame in 2014.

In his openly honest and heartfelt induction speech, he revealed much about his life that had previously been largely unknown. He mentioned that he grew up loving the wrestlers he saw on TV, but hated wrestling itself. The reason – his Father was a wrestler and preferred to be away performing instead of looking after his family. Ironically, he and his siblings would all become wrestlers, but Jake swore he would never treat his kids the same way his Father treated him.

So engrossed in playing his character on television and enjoying the life of a pro-wrestler on the road, he then admitted to doing exactly the same thing his Father did to him and his family. He neglected them and chose to wrestle instead. He loved the rush of being able to have control over the fans and their emotions while he did as brilliant act in the ring. It gave him that adrenaline rush that nothing else could.

He went on to talk about how his career went into tailspin as the years progressed. He had become so reliant on substances, and did not see his family, he felt he had nothing. Over time, many of his wrestling friends would pass away from different circumstances. He came to hate God, asking why not him, why them? He could not commit suicide as he did not want to hurt his family any more than he already had.

Knowing only how to do one thing, that being playing the part of Jake 'The Snake' Roberts, he came to feel his time in the wrestling world was over. And then something happened that would change his life. Diamond Dallas Page, his friend and colleague of many years, reached out to help him. Using his self-help and positive thinking attitude, he embarked on a project that came to be known as 'The Resurrection of Jake The Snake Roberts'. Jake was able to give up alcohol and drugs through a rehabilitation process. Not only that, but thanks to support and donations from fans online, he received surgery on his shoulder injury that had plagued him for years. He realised fans do still care about him, and he needed to get clean for his fans, his friends and especially, his family.

Jake wrapped up his hall of fame induction speech by saying that he felt ashamed and regret about his past life. He felt ashamed that God had given him so much talent, and he wasted a lot of it by being too incapacitated to use it. He felt ashamed for neglecting his family and not spending time with his children as they grew.

The most heartfelt and beautiful comments were saved for last. The cameras showed Jakes family observing the speech in the audience, where they looked extremely proud and delighted to be his children. Jake explained that his family are his heroes, and couldn't be happier to be reunited with them and his grandchildren as well. He took his young grandson onto the stage, a boy of less than two years old who has had multiple surgeries since birth, held him in his arms, and with tears of joy and hope he exclaimed "Vince, get your storywriters busy because at Wrestlemania 50 in twenty years, this kid will be there!"

He thanked his family for giving him a second chance, and the WWE for giving him that chance as well. A happy and proud man stood before us, no longer obsessed with his wrestling gimmick, or playing to the crowd, or getting an adrenaline rush for unfavourable substances. He stood before us a proud father, grandfather and family man. Jake Roberts has been resurrected in peace.

∞

The two stories given above have happy endings. Watching the Shawn Michaels/Undertaker story play out over the weeks and on the night itself showed me what can happen when one thing in life clouds over everything else, how you can stand to lose everything you have worked for in one moment. (In reality, Shawn had decided to retire from the business to spend more time with his family, at Church and in his new hobby of hunting – he went out losing to his favourite and most respected opponent).

Watching Jake's speech that night, it was spoken from the heart, pulling no strings, a rollercoaster of emotion. Being open and honest about his mistakes was breath taking to watch and listen to. He struck a chord with many that night. This was not a storyline on television, or Jake playing up to the camera for us. It was his story, of a man who had fought demons and won.

They lost what was important in life; they focused away from these for something of less significant in the grand scheme of things. They did not have their focus and priorities in order. Only through losing good things altogether did they come to realise what was most important.

We read in Matthew chapter 6, verse 33;

"But seek ye first the kingdom of God, and his righteousness; and all these things shall be added unto you."

The Lord commands us not to idle our time away. By doing that which matters most and focusing on the important matters in life, we can find happiness in doing so. Church members are taught to build ourselves up in the Kingdom of God, going by the example of Jesus Christ and encouraging others to do likewise. By doing so, we will establish a more peaceful life.

I admit here that I have been as foolish and as narrow minded as Shawn (in the story) and as Jake (in real life). Some years ago I lost sight of the true meaning of the Church and what my purpose was there. I forgot about the Savior, about his Atonement and about my commitments. I chose to seek that 'adrenaline rush' elsewhere and instead spent time away doing that which I knew in my heart was wrong. I felt sorry for myself and ashamed of myself, but figured that I could keep getting those temporary feelings of happiness each time, and perhaps the self-pity would depart eventually.

It was not until one Sunday afternoon, I woke up after a long and wild night out to find a text message from a friend at Church. He had sent it many hours before, asking 'Are you coming to Church, we miss you?' I had kept in touch with a few people from Church during my time away, but it was this message that struck a chord with me.

I went to the bathroom and looked at myself in the mirror. In it I saw a pathetic figure, who had gave up and quit, losing sight of what really mattered. I had become so consumed with having 'fun' on a Saturday night that I forgot about the importance of a Sunday morning. Instead of remembering the Savior and what he did, I was trying to remember what I had done the night before. I resolved to get myself back to Church and instead focus on my eternal perspective, on what mattered most. I knew in my heart that it was right and that happiness, true lasting joy could only come one way. It took a while, and a very heartfelt and honest conversation with someone who shall remain nameless (but they will know who they are), much prayer and some great friends, and I returned to the fold with a new and reinvigorated perspective.

We may lose some battles, but the war over the devil can, has been and will always be won. Shawn represented this, Jake represented this, and many others go through it daily and come to know it. It may not be easy, but it is worth it.

I end this chapter on a parable, and I credit John Ferrans for teaching this and allowing me to use it here. It regards a man who learns to appreciate and focus on that which is most important in life.

There was a man out shopping one day and came across a painting which he loved. He decided to buy it and hang it in his house for everyone to see.
When he got home, he tried hanging it in the living room above the fireplace, but was not happy with it there; he felt it did not look right. He tried it in the hallway, the dining room, the kitchen and the master bedroom, but could not find a place where he felt it was suited.
Disappointed, he took the painting back to the shop and asked for his money to be returned. He explained to the owner that he just could not find the right place for it, and it was not for him. He could not make it fit properly in his house.
The owner of the shop carefully explained to him that he could see how much the customer loved the painting and wanted him to keep it. He advised the man to take

everything out of his house, every last item leaving only empty rooms. Then hang the painting exactly where you can focus on it each day. Put everything else back in the house around it. Then, you will find happiness with that painting.

  The message here is clear, put what matters most in life first (family, Jesus Christ, health, worship etc.) and put everything else around it. You'll find that by doing so, the smaller and maybe less significant things fall into place easier than you expect.
  Just as Shawn realised at the end that his fans and his legacy were more important than one opponent, that Jake realised people do care and his family still love him, we can realise what is most important and focus on that. The Gospel of Jesus Christ allows for ultimate focus and guidance, and by studying it we will be forever focused.

∞

This chapter is dedicated to Jake 'The Snake' Roberts. His life, example and 'resurrection' have inspired me and many others to keep focused on that which matters most.

Chapter Seventeen

"I'm Sorry I Let You Down!"

The Parable Of Forgiveness

Matthew 6:12

"And forgive us our debts, as we forgive our debtors."

Our final chapter details a principle which has been touched on many times in the book but never fully explored until now – the miracle of forgiveness.

And fittingly, the book ends with a story involving Shawn Michaels in one of the absolute greatest matches of his entire career.

2003 was an exciting time on WWE television for a number of reasons. One being the storyline rivalry between the co-general managers of the Raw television program – Stone Cold Steve Austin and Eric Bischoff. The two went far back in history, to when Steve, who was then a rising star, was fired by WCW boss Eric Bischoff after suffering an injury. He further stated that Steve looked and acted to bland and would never make an impact on the wrestling business. How wrong he was.

Steve would work had and transform himself into the biggest star of the 90's, while Eric eventually saw WCW crumble around him and go out of business. Shortly after that, he took up the position of storyline general manager in WWE. Following the end of Steve's in ring career, he joined Eric as his partner to ensure he did not abuse his power. It was the classic wrestling story of good guy (Stone Cold Steve Austin) and bad guy (Eric Bischoff) without them actually stepping foot in the ring.

For months they tried to get along and run the show together (behind the scenes however they enjoyed working together and became friends), but in the end they could not make it work. It was proposed at Survivor Series pay-per-view that they both assemble a team of five men for a traditional survivor series elimination match – Team Austin vs Team Bischoff. There were stipulations added to the match, being that if Austin's team won he had the right to enforce the rules anyway he saw fit (meaning he could use violence where necessary – he is a wrestler after all) while if Bischoff's team won, Austin would be out of a job. These were hefty stipulations.

Team Austin consisted of Rob Van Dam, Booker-T, The Dudley Boys and Shawn Michaels. Eric Bischoff's team was comprised of Mark Henry, Scott Steiner, Chris Jericho, Christian and Randy Orton. All were great wrestlers and the ingredients for a very entertaining match.

The eliminations occurred at spaced intervals, giving the match a good story, with the crowd solidly behind team Austin (and both Austin and Bischoff were stationed ringside with their respective teams). Shawn was knocked into a ring post early in the match and bled heavily. Eventually it came down to unfavourable odds for Austin, leaving Shawn Michaels alone vs Christian, Chris Jericho and Randy Orton. Shawn was exhausted and had lost a lot of blood, but continued to fight in Steve's honour, his performance over the next ten minutes showed why he is a true legend in the ring. When hopes of him winning were almost dashed, he defeated both Christian and Chris Jericho, leaving just Randy Orton.

A young and eager Randy had a lot to prove here, and gave this best performance of his career at the time. However Shawn gained the advantage and was ready to complete the win...until Eric stepped in and kicked Shawn. Austin, seething at the interference of his colleague, entered the ring and proceeded to beat up Eric, knocking him up the aisle towards the arena entrance. While doing so, a wrestler named Batista entered the ring and executed a spinebuster on Shawn, knocking him out. The referee had been knocked down during the last few minutes of the match and failed to see this. Once recovered, Randy covered Shawn and won the match. Austin turned around just in time to see the pinfall. His career was over.

And this is the really emotional heart wrenching moment of the entire show that night.

Shawn did everything he could in the match, no man has ever wrestled so passionately on someone else's behalf the way Shawn did here. They were enemies once upon a time, but now there was a great respect between the two.

Shawn was left lying in the ring, blood covering his face and torso. Sweat was dripping from him and was obviously in a lot of pain. Steve entered the ring and looked at him. Bending down to speak to Shawn, we could see them say something to each other, most likely Shawn explaining about Batista. It was at this point we could see just how much blood Shawn had lost, it was all over the ring canvas. Shawn grabbed onto Steve's shirt and tugged at it, perhaps trying to help himself up but too weak to do so. As Austin rose back up, Shawn was able to get to his knees. We could see him mouth the words "I'm sorry". With that, Steve picked him up to his feet. Shawn said again "I'm sorry I let you down". As he said this, Steve reached out a hand and shook Shawn's hand, mouthing the words – "I forgive you" as the crowd applauded these two legends of the squared circle. They walked backstage together; in the knowledge that Shawn did everything he could that night for Steve Austin. It was a beautiful moment for any wrestling fan.

∞

The message here is simple; it is the joy of mercy and forgiveness. We are all human and make mistakes. We can slip up and as followers of Jesus Christ we will feel guilty for doing so. We may feel like we have let him down and saddened by our actions.

Just as Stone Cold was able to pick up Shawn, forgive him and recognise all that he had done, we can have a similar experience with the Savior.

Like Shawn in the match, we battle in our daily lives all the bad and evil of the world. We will give it all that we have, doing everything we can do overcome the evil, sometimes showing scars in the process.

And, like Batista sneaking in and catching Shawn when off guard, Satan too will catch us off when we least expect it.

As long as we have done all we can do to stay on the right side and be the best we can be, Jesus will at the last day look down at our battered body and bruised sole, we will be on our knees just as Shawn was, and ask for forgiveness.

And Jesus, seeing all that we have done in life, will pick us up in his arms saying the words – "It's OK, I forgive you". It is through him and by him that all sins may be forgiven. We are expected to do everything in our power to stay clean, and He will make up the rest.

Doctrine & Covenants 57:42 reads;

> "Behold, he who has repented of his sins, the same is forgiven, and I, the Lord, remember them no more."

And that is the greatest blessing and lesson of all. From the wrestling ring that is this mortal earth, we will walk together with Christ up from the ring and backstage into Heaven, where our glorious rewards await us.

Sharpshooters And Sermons

Epilogue

"We're Outta Time Folks!"

I've been asked a number of times throughout the years why I watch what they call a 'fake sport'. Why I, and thousands upon thousands of other fans sit and watch something that is made out to be real while it is no more than a staged show. In a wrestling fans eyes, it might be the most disrespectful and offensive thing you can say to them, and surely to the wrestlers themselves.

Wrestling is staged; we understand it is a show that is for our entertainment. Wrestling is choreographed, where the wrestlers work with each other to perform the moves without actually hurting each other. Wrestling is an art, where they design the match and the moves to have us in awe. Wrestling is a story, a battle of good vs evil, of redemption, of love, of passion, of will, of determination, of sacrifice and a pure desire to be the best and prove you are the best.

But what it is not is fake. It is far from it. They spend their lives in agony from all the slams to the mat, the bumping into each other, the jumping from the top rope. While it is choreographed, it's impossible not to feel pain and agony after doing it so long. They do it for each and every fan who loves to escape from reality for a few hours and be entertained, because they love the rush it gives them and they love to entertain.

Steve Austin did not break his neck for you to say 'It's all fake, he'll be running about tomorrow morning'. Shawn Michaels didn't wrestle in 1998 with a broken back and do it with such heart and determination for you to say 'He's just acting'. And Darren Drozdov didn't take a pile driver and become paralysed for you to laugh about how it's not 'real'.

Those that say it's not real – They are disrespecting thousands of men and women who take time away from families and homes, and put their bodies through immense pain and pressure to entertain those that appreciate it.

And at the end of the day, they all go back together and enjoy the rewards of being simply brilliant. They look out at their fans and they smile and say "Well it's really all worth it ain't it".

∞

Sadly, I am also asked a similar question in regards to Religion. Why am I spending my time focusing on something that they claim is just made up? Some say Christianity is just worshipping someone who was very intelligent and creative, but had no real powers.

I have always maintained that everybody is free to their own opinion and decision regarding Religious beliefs. There are many different types of Religion and ways of worshipping, and I respect all different beliefs and practices. I believe God has a plan for everyone – some will find joy in worshipping and some will not. Some will believe and some will not. And some will be respectful and some will not.

I believe there was a reason I met with the Missionaries from the LDS Church that day and this is where I am meant to be, that this is the truest and most correct Church on earth, that it is Christ's Church. And I deeply respect and admire any other Religion and see good in them all. I have friends from other faiths and while we may not agree fully on certain points of doctrine, but we agree on the goodness of Jesus Christ. To those that do not believe in Him, we can only invite to find out and see for themselves.

My final thought is that being a follower of Jesus Christ does not simply involve accepting him as the Savior and moving on with life. It is so much more. To requote John 13: 34-35, where Jesus is speaking to his disciples;

"A new commandment I give unto you, That ye love one another; as I have loved you, that ye also love one another. By this shall all men know that ye are my disciples, if ye have love one to another."

That is the ultimate message of any Religion, to love one another, thereby creating a peaceful environment for all concerned. People will slip up and make mistakes and even sometimes forget which side they are on, but it can be all be rectified because of Him.

Sharpshooters And Sermons

Sharpshooters And Sermons

The Make-A-Wish Foundation

A portion of the proceeds from the book will be donated to the Make-A-Wish Foundation. They exist for one reason, to grant magical wishes to enrich the lives of children fighting life threatening conditions. The charity is based in the UK and forms part of the worldwide foundation of the same name. It has existed here since 1986.

I decided whilst writing the book I would like to use part of the proceeds to help a chosen charity in their cause. The WWE has a long association with the charity in America, having their wrestlers meet children across the Nation to make their wish come true. John Cena and Mick Foley are two of their biggest ambassadors, with John having granted over one thousand wishes at the time of writing.

As this is a book based around wrestling, I could think of no better charity to donate too. I respect and admire what the charity sets out to do, and what the wrestlers and many other celebrities, companies and the public have done and will continue to do. Their work means a lot to these children and their families in times of need and uncertainty.

Sharpshooters And Sermons

Any comments or suggestions regarding the book are welcomed via the Facebook page.
Search "Sharpshooters And Sermons" and send a message.

Many thanks for reading.

Darren Kane
Manifesto 4:13 Productions
"Amazing – Yesterday, Now, Always!"

CPSIA information can be obtained
at www.ICGtesting.com
Printed in the USA
LVOW04s1541151115

462669LV00023B/1012/P

9 781508 431824